Do All Races Share In Salvation?

For Whom Did Jesus Christ Die?

By Pastor Dan Gayman

First Edition, 1985	**7,500 copies**
Revised Edition, 1995	**3,500 copies**
Revised Edition, 2012	**3,500 copies**

All Scripture references are from the Authorized King James Version of the Bible, unless otherwise noted.

The views expressed in this book are those of its author and do not necessarily reflect the views of any particular church or organization with whom the author may be affiliated.

Printed in the United States of America

Library of Congress Catalog Number: 95-095324

ISBN 9781468168587

Contents

FOREWORD

This book is written to the Christian remnant who resides as exiles in all corners of the earth. For those covenant seed of Abraham, Isaac, and Jacob who are seeking truth, this book is for you. This is not about who is right and wrong, who has sinned and who is free from error. This is a book about truth and an attempt to point the covenant people toward the truth of their God and His revealed will for their lives. For those who continue to have the instinct of self-preservation beating in their hearts, and for those who wish to preserve the racial integrity of their children and their children's children, this book has great merit. This book is for those who intuitively know that something is radically wrong with the multi-racial world now gathering on American shores. People who are weary of the theological dogmas that push for total integration, amalgamation, and fusion of the races in American society will be especially pleased to read this book.

It has become commonplace in America for people to believe that God and Scripture sanction a multi-racial society. Millions have assumed that the great mixing, amalgamation, and fusion of the races now underway in America must have the blessings of God and His Word. The idea of preserving the racial integrity of the various races occupying the American fatherland was long ago surrendered. Most people have walked through the wide gate and down the broad way of total integration and amalgamation of the races. Millions assume that God would be honored to find nothing left of the original separate and distinct races on earth. The push to erase all racial distinction and separa-tion is coming from every quarter of society. The United States Government has legislated racial integration and now pushes for total amalgamation of the races in every strata of American society.

The major denominations within the Western Church world are united in their efforts to bring about a total fu-sion of all races into one racial blend. What God created separate and distinct man purposes to remold into some-thing else. The humanists of this world are not content to let God and Scripture establish the perimeters and bound-aries of racial truth. They are determined, by whatever means necessary, to destroy the purity of every race and remake them all in man's demented image. So complete is this push to integrate and blend the races that the total power of the media, government, church, and educational systems are focused in this direction. Like a giant glacier plunging down the mountain side and crushing everything in its path, the builders and makers of the new world racial order have mobilized every institution of man to erase the color line and build this tower of Babel, a veritable fusion of all races into one blend. No power on earth seems capable of stop-ping this mad rush to racial oblivion.

This book is not intended to reform and educate those who are seeking to recreate God's world and the separate and distinct races that He placed on earth. These people are programmed from the cradle to do what they are doing. The racial programs of modern America are the harvest of blatantly false ideas that have been pushed in American society for the past one hundred fifty years. We are now reaping the bitter harvest of previous ideas planted in the hearts and minds of our people. A majority of people now living in America and the Western world have been born and reared on a humanist diet of racial integration and amalgamation. These people know nothing else. Vast numbers of them have mixed their gene pool with the blood of other races. For such people there is no hope. They are lost in this world, and they will be lost in the world to come. Time and history will witness their demise in the plan and purpose of God.

The purpose of this book is to arrest the attention of that small Christian remnant who seeks to follow the truth of God in a hostile world. This book will guide the minds and hearts of such people into the truth of Scripture and will provide the basis for their action now and in the days to come. These people need the assurance of God and Scripture that the racial integrity of every race is what God ordained. They need to know that the **original design** that God intended for every race is something that must be preserved. The Christian remnant needs to know that the future of their children is dependent upon the decisions they make today. Tomorrow will be too late. Time is of the essence. The rush to mix, amalgamate, and integrate is so great that no one is safe without great care being exercised to preserve racial purity. For those whose hearts are seeking after God, this book will be extremely helpful. It will convict them that the racial integrity that is already in their hearts is truly confirmed by their God and the truth of His Word.

The racial clouds that are gathering over America in this generation pose clear and present danger for the covenant people now living in this land. America is currently ingesting millions from the third world. The landscape of the Southwestern United States is already filled with Hispanics. Mexico has enlarged its borders to include Texas, New Mexico, Arizona, and Southern California. The western coastal areas of the nation are being peopled by Asians. Seattle and San Francisco are Asian cities. All major urban areas of the interior of the United States are teeming with millions of Negroids. Many of the largest interior cities of America belong to the Negro. Cuba, Haiti, Puerto Rico, and other islands of the Caribbean have moved north to consume Florida and much of Texas. For all practical purposes, America can be classified as a third world nation. The plummeting standards of living, the degenerating morals, and criminal violence attest to America's third world status. For millions, the reality of **third world status** has yet to be realized. The moment of truth will come when the squalor, disease, unemployment, crime, violence, sub-standard housing, and a crumbling infrastructure of the American nation are everywhere manifested. Third world horrors will strike home when people can no longer buy or acquire adequate food supplies and when the plunging living standards confine their children to the permanent status of minimum wage earning power.

If people ever do wake up, and many of them never will, the specter of a fully integrated society will be a permanent event in American history. Integration and fusion of the races can never be undone! The racial integrity of the covenant people has been built by generations who were fully committed to a segregated society. The pure Caucasians living today are pure because faithful ancestors believed in God and the truth of His Word. They faithfully preserved the integrity of their genetic history. It is sad to see people who will cast asunder a heritage of racial purity in the **sin** of miscegenation. The conception of one **out of kind** offspring can bring death to a family lineage. Some of the greatest names and families in the history of the Anglo-Saxon racial family are coming to an end in the terrible sin of **interracial dating and marriage.**

The children and youth of contemporary America are being cast into the caldron of racial amalgamation. Only a minority will survive the fires of interracial dating and marriage in the urban centers of America. The total force of the American educational system, the news media, the cinema, literary world, and the government are dedicated to a fusion of the races. Television networks provide a daily menu of race mixing. Worst of all, most parents either do not care, or they feel incapable of knowing what to do in the face of racial amalgamation. Caucasian parents send their racially pure daughters off to the university; to their utter dismay, they return with a black boyfriend! Racial barriers are being crossed in staggering numbers. What once was called shameful is now condoned in American society.

Every truth of God and the Bible has been wrenched from the minds of contemporary Americans. Few of them know what God and Scripture say about race. When the clergy speaks on this matter, it is only to give Biblical credence to a fully integrated and mixed society. Seldom, if ever, would a member of the American clergy lift his (or nowadays, *her*) voice in protest to the racial fusion now in progress. If an occasional parent draws a line and establishes a point beyond which their young people cannot go in terms of social integration of the races, they will be censored by their neighbors, rebuked in their community church, and ridiculed by the news media. Those who wish to build a fully integrated America will have nothing less than the complete fusion of the blood of all races. It is not enough to share equally in the economic resources of America. These people want the races to be one in blood, brains, and skin color. They want all lines of color and racial distinction removed from the scene of history. They want the demise of every distinct race and will accept nothing less.

The most painful aspect of the movement to build a fully integrated America is that the force of law is now behind it.

Statutory law and court decrees insure a program that will bring the ultimate demise of every pure race in America. A plethora of legislation and court decrees have marshalled the full power of the Federal government to attain a fully integrated, multi-racial society in America. Thousands of United States troops enforced the integration of American schools in Little Rock, Arkansas, in Montgomery, Alabama, and elsewhere at the beginning of this program of national genocide. A veritable army of Federal policemen stands ready to enforce the integration policies of the nation. A steady progression of events, initiated in the early nineteenth century, has moved America to the point of committing genocide against the culture bearing people of this nation.

It is too late to imagine any large scale roll back of the social programs that have turned America into a third world nation. Any hope of preserving the Caucasian population of this country has long since passed. The social agenda of the United States Government in the last half of the 20th century has forever ended the Caucasian fatherland in the American landscape.

With this pessimistic view before us, what can the Christian remnant do to preserve a future for their children? There are some things that we can do; this is the real purpose for writing this booklet. With the unfailing help and aid of Jesus Christ, the assistance of the Holy Spirit, the truth of Scripture, and a resolve that we can preserve the racial integrity of a Christian remnant, this treatise is published. There are a number of things the covenant people can do in this late hour. Please consider the following steps as vital to insuring the racial integrity of the Christian remnant now living in America and other nations of the formerly Western Christian culture.

Firstly, we can be armed with the truth of God and Scripture. We need to know what God's moral will has to say about this verboten subject. That the clouds of Biblical illiteracy can be dissipated is the prayer of this author. We must get into the Word of God and know what Scripture has to say. Secondly, the Christian remnant must purpose to stand guard over their children and preserve the racial genes of the present and future generations. Only when God-fearing people covenant and combine themselves together in Jesus Christ and pledge to live according to His Word can they survive the racial confusion of our generation. This requires that people give careful attention to their geography and other vital factors. They must remove their children from the public schools and provide alternative Christian education. They must remove their children from the proximity of the mixed multitude now collecting in the urban areas of the land. They must resolve to take wives for their sons, and husbands for their wives, from acceptable ethnic seed of their race. The covenant people must hold on to the twin pillars of **faith and race.** Faith in Jesus Christ and obedience to His Law will insure the racial integrity of the covenant people.

America is making a place for every religion and ethnic group now swarming our land. In the much applauded democracy of contemporary America, much praise is given to the great diversity of race, religion, and language. The Christian remnant must insist on retaining their place in this multi-racial society. If a place is allowed for the Jews and the Talmud, the Moslems and the Koran, the Moonies, the Buddhists, and whatever other religion and ethnic group you can name, there also must be reserved a place for the children of the Preamble people. I refer to the people now living who represent the posterity of those who wrote the United States Constitution. I refer to the children of those who fought the American War of Independence, or whose ancestors later arrived on the soil of America and helped to settle and develop the American nation.

By the unfailing help of Jesus Christ, the Christian remnant will survive. They will not succeed because of their goodness, righteousness, or because they deserve to be saved from the Tower of Babel now being built in America. They will survive because they are the people of the Book, the seed of Abraham, Isaac, and Jacob. They are the people whose existence on earth was to endure as long as the sun, the moon, and the stars endured in the heavens (Jeremiah 31:35-37). Indeed, these are the people whose names and seed were to survive as long as the new heavens and the new earth were to endure (Isaiah 66:22). These are the people for whom Jesus Christ died (Matthew 1:21, Luke 1:54-55, 68, 72). These are children of the covenants and promises of the Bible. They are the people whom God our Father marked in election before the world began (Ephesians 1:4,5). These are the people whose kinsman was and is Jesus Christ, the Son of God. These are the people called the lost sheep of the House of Israel. These are the people whom Jesus Christ came to seek and save (Matthew 15:24, Luke 19:9-10, Romans 9:4-5, Romans 10:1, Galatians 4:4-5, Acts 5:31, James 1:1, and I Peter 1:1-2).

There is one factor that towers above all others in regards to building a multi-racial nation in the American landscape. That factor concerns the inclusion of all races as being proper subjects for salvation by faith in Jesus Christ. Beginning in the early 17th century, the clergy in England, Scotland, and Europe became consumed with the idea of exporting Christianity to the third world nations. So compelling was this foreign missionary program that it became the primary obsession with major denominations in Christendom. As missionaries from the British Isles, Europe, and America fanned out across India, Africa, and the Far East, major developments began to happen. These foreign missions were to have awesome results in the ensuing years. Mission programs from the Caucasian Christian world awakened and aroused the third world people to the affluence of the Western world. This provided the impetus for a tidal wave of third world people to migrate toward the homelands of missionaries who had come to give them the Gospel. Foreign missions may be considered a major factor in the movement of the third world toward Europe, the British Isles, Scandinavia, America, Canada, and Australia.

A major concern of this thesis regards the exporting of the **Gospel of Jesus Christ** to the third world. Is there a Biblical sanction for foreign missions to the non-white world? Does the blood of Jesus Christ reach beyond the limits of God's election? Can salvation be inclusive of the whole world? Did Jesus Christ die for the elect, or for all the world? How far does the blood of Jesus Christ extend? Is there salvation in Jesus Christ for all races? Do all races share a common origin in Adam, the fall, and in their subsequent need to be saved? Did Jesus Christ take the seed of Abraham in the incarnation? Or, did He take on the seed of every race in the miracle of the incarnation? Did He come to redeem only those who were under the penalty of the law? Did He come to extend salvation to those who were never under law? Were all races placed under the penalty of law? Does original sin apply only to Adam's race, or does birth sin extend to all others outside of Adam's race? Is there Biblical support for the foreign missions to the third world? Is Christianity a multi-racial religion? Is it Biblical for Christians to worship in a multi-racial congregation? All of these questions and more will be explored in this booklet.

Thank you for taking this perilous journey. Not many people in this generation are willing to explore the issue before us. Most people prefer to rest content, bury their heads in the sand, and pray that no one will bother them with the question of race and faith. May JEHOVAH, the covenant God of Israel, be glorified by the printing of this booklet. And may all who read this booklet be willing to submit their souls to God our Father by faith in Jesus Christ and turn from dead works to repentance and newness of life in the power of the Holy Spirit. In the context of this foreword, can we examine the question *Do All Races Share in Salvation?* The remainder of this booklet will explore this question. Thank you for the spirit of humility and the willingness to allow God and His Word to be the only standard for your life in this present evil world.

Pastor Dan Gayman

1

AN HISTORICAL PERSPECTIVE

The most explosive theological debate in the history of the Christian Church is now underway. This great debate has been gathering intensity since the post-Protestant Reformation era of history. With the third-world invasion of the United States of America and the Western world in general, the issue is developing into a theological inferno of intense concern by Bible scholars and Christian laymen throughout the world. The question of a multi-racial Church never entered the minds of the Churchmen who occupied the pulpits and altars of the Living Church from the days of the Apostles to the time of the Protestant Reformation. Viewing history in its totality, multi-cultural thinking is new. Only on rare occasions, as with the builders of the Tower of Babel (Genesis 11), have men sought to promote a one-world, multi-cultural, pluralistic society.

In the years that followed the Protestant Reformation (beginning in the early 1500's), the discovery and exploration of lands beyond the boundaries of Christian Europe and Western Asia introduced for the first time in the history of Christianity the question of exporting Christianity to the non-white world. A quick survey of Church history confirms the fact that until the dawning of the 17th century, Christianity was confined to the Caucasian population of Western Asia, Europe, Scandinavia and the British Isles. The idea of a multi-racial Christian Church was not an issue in the first fifteen hundred years of the Christian Church. Not until Caucasian Christian Europe was aware of the existence of the non-white world was any thought given to foreign missions. The Renaissance not only initiated a revival of Greek and Roman culture, but also it caused Christian minds to meditate upon the possibility of taking the gospel to the third world. The ships that were plying the seas in search of new trade routes and markets in the early 1600's were also taking white Christian missionaries to distant lands.

The discovery and exploration of the non-white world by Roman Catholic, Spanish, and Portuguese sailors, explorers, and missionaries in the early 1500's was followed in the 1600's and 1700's by a legion of foreign missions from white Christian Europe to the non-white world of Africa, Asia, India, and Latin America. Beginning in the early 1600's and continuing to this very day, the exporting of the Christian religion to the non-white world has been the primary occupation of Christian Churchmen. The clergy, laymen, and missionary societies, throughout England, Scotland, Wales, Ireland, Scandinavia, Europe, and the United States of America, were zealous to plant foreign missions among the non-white populations of the earth. For fifteen hundred years the Christian Church knew only the color white. A quick check into the history of foreign missions will show that it was not until the beginning of the 17th century that any Churchman in the Western world entertained the idea of a multi-racial Christian religion.

In 1622, the **Congregation for the Propagation of the Faith** was launched by the Roman Catholic Church (this was a foreign mission program). In 1641, **The Petition for**

Propagating the Gospel in America and West Indies was launched from England. In 1698, the **Society for Promoting Christian Knowledge** was launched by the Church of England (this was still another foreign missionary program). In 1701, **The Society for the Propagation of the Gospel in Foreign Parts** was launched by the Church of England. August Hermann Francke (D-1727) was a leader of Pietism among Lutherans in Europe and was an advocate of foreign missions. Thomas Chalmers, a Scottish Churchman (1780-1847), promoted foreign missions. In 1785, Andrew Fuller published *The Gospel Worthy of All Acceptation*, and this fueled the fire for foreign missions.

In 1786, the Wesleyan Conference sent Thomas Coke to India. Coke was committed to evangelizing the non-white population of India. In 1792, a **Baptist Missionary Society** was formed in England and led by William Carey and John Thomas. In 1795, the Methodist Church succeeded from the Church of England and pushed foreign missions to the non-white world. In the same year, the **London Missionary Society** was formed. In 1799, the **Church Missionary Society** was formed, and the **Religious Tract Society** was organized. In 1804, the **British and Foreign Bible Society** was founded. Throughout the 19th century and on into the 20th century, foreign mission programs continued to proliferate throughout the Christian world. Today, almost every major denomination in the Christian world has a foreign mission program.

The preoccupation with foreign missions has consumed the Christian world for the past 200 years. The harvest of this foreign mission program has resulted in the present invasion of our Western Caucasian world with a flood of non-white aliens from Asia, India, Africa, and Latin America. Every nation in the Western world is now under alien invasion. Nothing has done more to facilitate and encourage the migration of the third world to the Caucasian West. The third world people have simply followed their mission leaders back to their affluent lands.

With the growing presence of so many millions of nonwhites from the colored races of Africa, India, Asia, and Latin America, the Christian Church has become multiracial. In spite of this fact, Christianity continues to reach out to the non-white world. Even the Mormon Church, not generally considered a part of historical Christianity, has joined the mad race to seek non-whites to fill their pews and lead their priesthood. (This change in Mormon doctrine took place in 1978 when a cornerstone teaching of the church was changed by their leadership). Leading churchmen of every denomination are breaking their religious necks to foster and promote foreign missions throughout the non-white world. The situation has now reached a total crisis in every nation of the West. The wealth, resources, and infrastructure of Europe, the British Isles, and the United States are being pushed to the limits by the growing numbers of third world people recruited to the West by Christian missionaries.

Will Christianity be able to survive this onslaught? Will the faith once delivered to the saints survive this infusion of non-white blood? Will a multi-racial Christian Church be the tolling of the death bells for the Christian Faith? Can the Christian religion seek to be multi-racial and continue to claim the Bible and a God/Man named Jesus Christ? Has a multi-racial Church turned the theology of Christianity into a shambles? The time has come for all true Christians to set aside misplaced love and pity and look directly at the single greatest question facing the Christian world today. The pulpits of Christianity, ablaze with the zeal of foreign missions for the past three hundred and fifty years, are now reaping the harvest of their labors. Foreign missions failed to raise the Christian standard in the home of the natives. The natives have followed their Christian teachers back to the sponsoring nation. Foreign missions may end up being one of the most tragic programs ever fostered in the name of Jesus Christ and Christianity.

THE CHRISTIAN REMNANT

There is a remnant of Bible scholars, ministers, pastors, teachers and laymen throughout America and the Western world who hold fast to the idea that Christianity is the religion of the Caucasian race. Moreover, there are those who claim that Christianity cannot survive the horrors of what a multi-racial Church will bring about in the immediate and future generations of white Christians. There is a tiny remnant of churchmen in America and the Christian West who hold to the faith and tenants of Apostolic Christianity as it was taught by Jesus Christ and the apostles. These people reject the foreign mission programs initiated by various denominations in the 17th and 18th centuries. This remnant has its racial origins among the Anglo-Saxon-Germanic-Scandinavian-Slavonic kindred people of the earth. These people hold to the idea of Christianity as it was practiced up to the time of the Protestant Reformation. This Christian remnant continues to believe that Christianity cannot be a multi-racial faith. Their belief arises out of sacred scripture and the precedents established during the first 1500 years of Christian Church history. These people are holding to the Christianity that was molded and forged by Jesus Christ, the apostles, and the early Church fathers.

The Christian remnant does not wish to force its opinion on other people. They only demand a fair and reasonable place in American society to believe and practice what has always been true in historic Christianity. Racial purity has always been a cornerstone of the Christian religion. The Christian remnant does not wish to alter the **original design** of the Creator. We recognize that there is a growing trend to build a multi-cultural, multi-racial society in America and that this racial pluralism is fostered and encouraged from the pulpits of Christendom. We are not asking that those who want to enter the genocide of their race be stopped from doing so. We are simply saying that we will have no part in the **miscegenation** now being promoted in the name of Christ and Christianity. We only ask for the liberty to live and practice our Christianity as taught in the sacred Scripture by Christians for the first fifteen hundred years of the living Church. If others choose to mix, integrate, and amalgamate their genetics in a fusion of all races, so be it. As for the Christian remnant, however, we will have no part of it.

If the Jews can promote **Judaism** and their belief in the Talmud among their people, the Christian remnant ought to be able to promote their faith and belief in the same landscape. If there is room in America for the **Moslems** and the Koran, there should be a place for remnant Christians of the Bible. If the Hindus can minister the Vedas to the adherents of **Hinduism**, remnant Christians ought to be able to follow the Bible and their leader, Jesus Christ. If the Buddhists, Moonies, and a vast assortment of other religions can find liberty to promote their faith among their folk, is there not a place for the Christian remnant? Moreover, let it be known that the people making up the Christian remnant are descended from ancestors who have been on American soil for many generations. We are not newcomers to the American continent.

There is a growing trend for Churchmen within the fold of the Christian remnant to compromise their racial posi-

tion and surrender to the prevailing winds of doctrine blow-
ing throughout the Christian world. More and more churchmen are willing to erase the color line and concede to building a multi-racial Church. Christian people who love Jesus
Christ, the Bible, and their children are concerned about
where a multi-racial Christianity is taking us. These people
want answers, and they deserve to be heard. Do all races
share in salvation? Does the Bible warrant a multi-racial
Church? Is Christianity a faith for all races? Is God color
blind? Does God segregate and discriminate? Does the blood
of Jesus Christ redeem all races? How far did the atonement of Jesus Christ extend? These questions must be
answered.

Time is running out! Ministers are beginning to buckle
under the pressure of a growing multi-racial media blitz in
America and throughout the Western world. The color line
is being erased by more and more ministers within the
Christian remnant. Men are losing their convictions of racial truth as they surrender to public pressure. Christian
laymen wrestle with this problem in prayer before God.
Does God want a multi-racial Church? Is Christianity a
religion for all races? What does the Bible teach? The greatest
test of the Christian religion in two thousand years is now
before us. Will inspired churchmen step forward and meet
this challenge? For the sake of our children and the faith
once delivered to the saints, let us pray that they do!

This treatise is intended to be the beginning of a theological foundation upon which the Christian family, ministers, teachers, pastors, and laymen can establish a position on this tremendous problem. This booklet will not attempt to address all the issues that can be raised in such a
discussion. It is written in the fervent hope that it can provide godly, Christian clergy and parents with a Biblical
foundation to practice racial purity in the living Church.

Any Church that sponsors a foreign mission should give immediate consideration to disbanding that program. Christian parents must flee any church that encourages and condones miscegenation. Finally, remnant Christians should nail down their minister's position on this subject. What does he believe about the blood of Jesus Christ? Does he believe and teach that salvation includes all the world? Do not follow a multitude to do evil. Draw your lines and establish truth in your life. Your children and your children's children will be forever blessed if you do.

2

STILLING TROUBLED WATERS

Any discussion of the subject at hand (do all races share in salvation?) is likely to arouse a strong, emotional response. People have been made to feel extremely sensitive about race because of incessant bombardment by the news media for a full generation and more. The American educational system is keyed to racial sensitivity. The pulpits of American churches are ablaze with soothing sermons to calm the troubled waters of racial tension. The United States Government is dedicated to removing racism from the landscape of America. The United States military force has been transformed by racial sensitivity. Any subject you can think of can be openly discussed and debated in American society, *except for race*. As a topic, race is verboten in contemporary America. If, however, you wish to discuss the virtues of Jews, Asians, Negroids, or other non-Caucasian ethnic groups, feel free! Any talk about the virtues of the Caucasian race is forbidden. You simply dare not mention anything positive about them, or you will be charged with racism. (Have you noticed it applies only to those who speak out in favor of whites?) A person of color can do just about anything without fear of intimidation or being charged with racism.

Reverse discrimination is a growing social phenomena in American society. More and more white males are going to court to reaffirm their position in the American workplace. The legislatures, courts, colleges, universities, and the typical work place have gone so far in their efforts to create a non-discriminating climate for the non-whites that growing numbers of white males are struggling for survival. Caucasian males are now the subjects of gross discrimination in American society. Women of every race and all non-white males are given preferential treatment in almost every aspect of American society. Affirmative action has almost destroyed the American work place. Employers are crippled by the limitations imposed by the racial and gender quotas established under color of law. The sensitive subject of race has been handed to the Caucasian male in a very insensitive manner.

An open and candid dialogue with the readers of this book may be in order before setting forth the Biblical presuppositions that will determine the answer to the question *do all races share in salvation*. The following statement is intended to set the tone on the matter of race for those who will read this booklet and seek to build their lives on truth. Please take time to consider the following rationale so that you may better understand the Biblical case about salvation and the people for whom Jesus Christ died. Give careful and prayerful thought to that which follows and let these thoughts become the basis for understanding that portion of the book which will follow.

This book is not a book about hate. It is about truth. In the beginning, God created all races separate and distinct. God considered everything that He had made and found it to be very good (Genesis 1:31). Every race bears the mark of God's ownership. Each race was created according to the **original design** of the Creator God. Every race was uniquely endowed by the Creator to fulfill its destiny in the cycle of life and God's plan for the earth. Each race was appointed the boundaries of their habitation and accorded their place on earth. The Creator placed the Asians in the Far East. He planted the Negroids in Africa near the equator where they are environmentally at home. The Caucasian race was placed in the northern latitudes of Europe and North America where they find themselves at home.

God established the earth to be the home for all races. But, notice that He established racial **separatism** as the means by which every race would retain their **original design.** God is a God of segregation and preservation. Man, seeking to remake the creation in his fallen image, seeks for integration and the ultimate destruction of the original design placed in every race. The Creator purposed for every race to be preserved and to retain all its unique qualities that make them separate and distinct. It is not my intention to elevate one race above another, to praise one at the expense of the other, or to diminish the greatness that the Creator God established in every race. There is no intent whatever to demoralize any race in this book. To the contrary, I wish to preserve the very best that the Creator God intended for each race. I wish God's best for the Asians (yellow Mongoloids), Negroids (blacks), and the Caucasians. Nothing will be gained from robbing any race of the blessings which the Creator intended. I pray that every race could be preserved in its original design.

A brief mention of form, value, and function of the various races may be in order. This should aid in a better understanding and outlook on the broad subject before us.

Form: In form, every race is created different. A careful review of the Caucasoid, Negroid, and Mongoloid races reveals a tremendous range of biological, psychological, mental, and other differences. In form, then, every race bears the mark of God's distinctive ownership. The flesh, bones, and blood structure of the races are different. Brain weight and composition varies from race to race. Skin color, blood type and composition, bone structure, and brain weight, size, and convulsions are all unique in every race. It is not my purpose to argue in favor of the form which God gave to each of the races He created. Everything that God made He called very good (Genesis 1:31). In that sense, we must rest content that in form, every race bears the racial type that God purposed for them. What God has purposed let not man change through race mixing. The **law of kind after his kind**, mentioned ten times in Genesis 1, forbids the alteration of the form which the Creator intended for every race to preserve.

Value: The value of every race was established by the Creator God. Since God purposed a special mission and destiny for every race, we must argue for the value of every race. Every race is uniquely important and vital to the total purpose for which God created life, the earth, and the fullness thereof. The Creator God placed His own value on every race. He created them precisely the way He wanted them. We must submit to the idea that in value as in form, there is no equality. **God made all races different and for different reasons.** It is not for man to add to or subtract from the value which the Creator gave to every race. We must simply rest content in knowing that every race has its own special and unique role to play in God's unfolding plan. Self-acceptance of the race into which you were born is a critical need in the life of every living being. To deny the value of the race into which we are born is to challenge the work of the Creator God.

Function: In function each race moves forward with a totally different agenda. One race may excel in a given activity while another race functions better in something else. In function, there is no equality. Each race is equipped with those unique genetic qualities that enable it to excel at those areas intended by the Creator God. One race may be adept at abstract, creative thinking. They simply exercise and use the unique qualities of the brain. They are thinkers! Another race may have been afforded physical prowess and qualities of endurance. Still another race may have been given peculiar qualities that enable members of this race to excel at given tasks. In function, every race performs in a totally different way. If there is variation in form and function within the members of each unique race, consider how vast these differences are between the separate and distinct races which the Creator made!

Any attempt to amalgamate and mix the races (Caucasoid, Mongoloid, and Negroid) will destroy the **value, form, and function** of every race. No greater sin can be committed in God's creation than to take what God has created and destroy their value, form, and function. *Miscegenation is a sin* which alters and destroys the original design of every race and brings its creative and productive life cycle to an end. The failure of man to preserve the value, form, and function of every race will have awesome consequences for the offspring of future generations. Having been robbed of their unique genetic differences, they will live in a state of **racial confusion** and thus be incapable of performing in the form and function designed by the Creator God. **What God has created, let no man recreate.**

RACE AND RELIGION

It may come as a surprise to many that the Creator God gave to every race a unique capacity to know God in a different way. All races can know God as **Creator,** and they can and do worship Him in their unique way. The Negroids have always worshipped the Creator in variant forms of voodooism, ancestral spirits, and physical objects of nature. The Negroids can and do worship God as Creator. They do not worship the Creator in the same manner and style as the Mongoloids. This distinct race has their own method of knowing and worshipping the Creator. Caucasians have still another means of knowing and worshipping God. The vast differences with which the various races worship God is well known by **anthropologists** but is all too often forgotten by those who are out to convert the world to the method by which the Caucasian race worships and knows God.

Historically, the Negroids have followed the patterns established in the earliest known history of their race. Every attempt to alter and change their method of knowing and worshipping God has not remained permanent with them. When left alone to pursue their preferences, they always revert to the gods of their ancestors. The same will be true for all other races. When Caucasians are converted to the gods of the heathen, they do not remain satisfied. They will, in time, forsake their heathen gods and begin to search for the God of their fathers. When you seek to orient the mind of the Negroid toward the God of the Caucasians, it will not last long. **Every race was created to know their Creator in a different way and by a different means.** Please keep this in mind as you answer the question *do all races share in salvation.* Consider the great variety of religious preferences now abounding on our planet. Consider the various forms of voodooism that are followed in the Sub-Saharan African nations. Think carefully about the Hindus and their adaptation to the Vedas and the god they call Brahman. Give consideration to the proclivity of Arabs to their god Allah, and to their bible, the Koran.

Stop and ponder the manner in which the Oriental world panders to their gods. All cultures and races seem to have a different flare for knowing and worshipping God. When left to themselves, all of these races revert to the gods of their ancestors.

Why do we insist on casting all the races of the earth into the mold of Christianity? In the same sense that the Moslem faith is for the Arabs, Christianity is the faith of the Caucasians. In the same way that Orientals cling to **Buddha**, Caucasians cling to **Jesus Christ.** The typical Arab is just as sincere in his search for **Allah** as the Caucasian is for **Jesus Christ.** The gods of Voodoo are just as important to the Zulus as Jesus Christ is for the Caucasian. It is most unfortunate that Caucasians are born thinking that they must mold the religious preferences of other races into the mold of Christianity. It may be difficult for some people to understand, but this is true: **Christianity is the religion of the Caucasian race.**

Any attempt to wean other races from their gods and religion is a step backward and an attempt to recreate the world which God made. Moreover, when non-whites are recruited into Christianity, they quickly mold their new found Christianity into the image of their cultural gods. Non-white races are content with Christianity only after they have recast this new religion in the image of their own gods and ancestral faith. After **four hundred years** of evangelizing portions of Africa, Asia, India, and other regions of the earth, these native races remain surprisingly loyal to the gods of their own cultural creation. They really do not want the God of the Caucasian race. They are far more interested in the material abundance of the Caucasian world than they are the God who is worshipped in the Christian West.

Moreover, recruits into the Christian faith from non-white races generally seek to remake the Bible in the image of their own cultural gods and family lineage. Hence, the Bible, a book written to, for, and about Caucasian Adamite, Hebrew, Israelite, Christian people, is modified and rewritten to fit the more pleasing cultural history and gods of the people who are trying to force themselves into the mold of the Christian West. Not content to accept the Bible as historically written, they immediately go to work with revisionist ideas in mind. For many of those non-whites recruited into the Christian faith, the only acceptable Bible is one that is reworked in the cultural and racial image of their own people. It is painfully obvious that Caucasian Christians would be much better off seeking converts from their own racial and cultural background. By what Scriptural authority does the Christian West seek to evangelize and make converts from people who have never embraced the God and Bible of Christianity throughout all their history? And since these people will, if left to themselves, return to their cultural gods and religious customs, why expend so much time in evangelism with them?

Many are the Christian evangelists and missionaries from the Christian West who have come to the end of their careers with despondent hearts for the pitiful harvest of souls witnessed among the non-white people of the earth. Consider that since the days of David Livingstone (1813-1873) and Sir Henry Morton Stanley (1841-1904), Christian missionaries from the West have been seeking to convert the Negroid tribes of Africa. A never ending procession of Christian missionaries have packed their bags for some particular state in Africa. Vast amounts of money have been expended to Christianize the black population of Africa. Now nearing the end of two hundred years, the great black populous of sub-Sahara Africa remains in variant forms of Voodooism, their ancestral religion.

In conclusion, can we not give careful consideration to what God and Scripture have to say about converting the world to Jesus Christ? Did God intend for Christianity to be a religion that was peculiar to one people on earth? Do the sheep for whom the Bible was written to, for, and about, hear the voice of a stranger? Is there something in the genetic make up of every race that gives them a religious preference? Is the God who wrote the Bible color blind? Does the Creator still know what He created and for what purpose? How much latitude will we give to the God who wrote the Bible? Must we remake God in our image so that we can do as we please with His Word? Will every race not have a better future if we leave unchanged what God created and purposed?

With this very brief outline in mind, we are ready to proceed with some important word definitions in our theological quest, *do all races share in salvation?*

3

WORD DEFINITIONS

In seeking to answer the question **"Do all races share in salvation?"** it is necessary to define some important words. Before addressing these definitions, some preface remarks will help us have a proper frame of mind for this study. Firstly, we are reminded by St. Paul in I Corinthians 8:2, *"And if any man think that he knoweth any thing, he knoweth nothing yet as he ought to know."* Secondly, the words of John should keep us humble. *"...A man can receive nothing, except it be given him from heaven."* Thirdly, we clearly know that only they who have eyes to see and ears to hear will move forward in understanding this important subject. *"Who hath ears to hear, let him hear"* *(Matthew 13:9)*. Fourthly, Scripture is clear that only by the power of a sovereign God can we both will and do what we should do. We can only understand the issue before us if God wills for us to know. *"For it is God which worketh in you both to will and to do of his good pleasure"* *(Philippians 2:13)*. Finally, only through the work of the Holy Spirit can a believer come to the truth. If the Holy Spirit does not guide us, we cannot know truth. *"Howbeit when he, the Spirit of truth, is come, he will guide you into all truth: for he shall not speak of himself; but* *whatsoever he shall hear, that shall he speak: and he will shew you things to come"* (John 16:13).

It is in the fear of God and in concern for His truth that this study is undertaken. All the wisdom of the world is indeed foolishness with God (I Corinthians 3:19). Even the foolishness of God is wiser than all the wisdom of men (I Corinthians 1:25). It is not my intention to ignore the research and teachings of others who have looked into this matter. We have, over many years, given careful consideration to the question of how salvation is to be appropriated. It is my desire to give all the counsel of God's Word as we understand it (Acts 20:27) on this urgent matter. May the Holy Spirit anoint afresh all who would seek to know the truth. We come before God our Father by faith in Jesus Christ and pray for the Holy Spirit to make His presence known to all who will study this urgent theological question.

DEFINITION OF WORDS

Before stating the presuppositions that will undergird this study, several significant words need to be defined. Included among these are *election, redeem, redeemed, redemption, and salvation.* Let us look at each of these before building our presuppositions for this study.

ELECTION: *Elect* appears in the Bible seventeen times, while *election* appears six times. **Israelites are the elect of JEHOVAH.** Note this verse found in Isaiah 45:4: *"For Jacob my servant's sake, and Israel mine elect, I have even called thee by thy name: I have surnamed thee, though thou hast not known me."* The word *elect* in this passage is from a Hebrew root word #972 and #977 in **Strong's Exhaustive Concordance.**

#977 is *baw-kheer'* from #977 select: choose, chosen, chosen one, elect.

#977 is *baw-khar'*: a prim. root; to try, (by imp.) select: acceptable, appoint, choose, (choice) excellent, join, be rather, require.

Webster's 1828 Dictionary of the English Language says this about the word *elect*: "One chosen or set apart; applied to Christ. *"Behold my servant, whom I upheld; mine elect, in whom my soul delighteth"* (Isaiah 42:1). 2. Chosen or designated by God to salvation; predestinated to glory as the end, and to sanctification as the means; usually with a plural signification, the elect. *"Shall not God avenge his own elect?"* (Luke 18:7). *"If it were possible, they shall deceive the very elect"* (Matthew 24:24). *"He shall send his angels...and they shall gather his elect from the four winds"* (Matthew 24:31). 3. Chosen; selected; set apart as a peculiar church and people; applied to the Israelites (Isaiah 45:4).

In the New Testament, St. Paul designates Israel as being chosen in the election of God the Father. The word *election* appears in Romans 5:11 and Romans 11:7; on both occasions the word is being applied to Israel. St. Paul uses the word *election* in Romans 11:28: *"As concerning the gospel, they are enemies for your sakes: but as touching the election, they are beloved for the fathers' sake."* St. Paul emphasizes the importance of election in Romans 9:11: *"(For the children being not yet born, neither having done any good or evil, that the purpose of God according to election might stand, not of works, but of him that calleth;)"* In all of the above cited Scriptures, the word *election* in **Strong's Exhaustive Concordance to the Bible** is root word #1589 and #1586. In every case where this word appears in the Book of Romans, it refers specifically to Israel. Moreover, no other people in Scripture are ever designated as the elect or being in the election of God.

#1589 is *ek-log-ay* from #1586, select, by impl. favorite: chosen, elect. #1586 is *ek-leg-om-ahee*, to select: make choice, choose (out), chosen.

The following definitions for the word *election* appear in **Webster's 1828 Dictionary of the English Language.**

"Election, The act of choosing; choice; the act of selecting one or more from others. Hence appropriately, 2. The act of choosing a person to fill an office or employment, by any manifestation of preference, as by ballot, uplifted hands or via voice; as the election of a king, of a president, or a mayor. 3. Choice; voluntary preference; free will; liberty to act or not. It is at his election to accept or refuse. 4. Power of choosing or selecting. Davies. 5. Discernment; discrimination; distinction. To use men with much difference and election is good. Bacon. 6. In **theology,** divine choice; predetermination of God, by which persons are distinguished as objects of mercy, become subjects of grace, are sanctified and prepared for heaven. *There is a remnant according to the election of grace" (Romans 11:5).*"

In all their usages in the Bible where they refer to salvation, the words *elect* and *election* apply only to Israelites.

The words *redeem, redeemed, and redemption* appear in Scripture a number of times. *Redeem* appears in all the following Scriptures in the Old Testament, and in every case, the word is #6299 in **Strong's Exhaustive Concordance to the Bible.** Root word #6299 in Hebrew is *Paw-daw'*, a prim. root; to sever, i.e. ransom; to release, preserve; Redeem(ed) rescue.

"And what one nation in the earth is like thy people, even like Israel, whom God went to redeem for a people

to himself,..." *(II Samuel 7:23)*. *"And what one nation in the earth is like thy people Israel, whom God went to redeem to be his own people,..."* *(I Chronicles 17:21)*. *"Redeem Israel, O God, out of all his troubles"* *(Psalm 25:22)*. *"And he shall redeem Israel from all his iniquities"* *(Psalm 130:8)*.

Strong gives the following definition for *redeem* as it appears in Galatians 4:5 in the Greek New Testament: #1805 is *ex-ag-or-ad'-zo*, meaning to buy up, ransom, rescue from loss, redeem. *"To redeem them that were under the law, that we might receive the adoption of sons"* *(Galatians 4:5)*.

Redeem in **Webster's 1828 Dictionary of the English Language** is defined as follows: "10. In theology, to rescue and deliver from the bondage of sin and the penalties of God's violated law, by obedience and suffering in the place of the sinner, or by doing and suffering that which is accepted in lieu of the sinner's obedience. *"Christ hath redeemed us from the curse of the law, being made a curse for us"* *(Galatians 3:13 and Titus 2:14)*.

The word *redeemed* as used in Exodus 15:13, Isaiah 62:12, Psalm 77:15, and elsewhere is root word #1350 in **Strong's Hebrew Concordance.** #1350 is *gaw-al'*, a prim. root to redeem, to be the next of kin (and as such to buy back a relative's property, purchase, ransom, redeem. *"Thou in thy mercy hast led forth the people which thou hast redeemed: thou hast guided them in thy strength unto thy holy habitation"* *(Exodus 15:13)*. *"And they shall call them, The holy people, The redeemed of the LORD: and thou shalt be called, Sought out, A city not forsaken"* *(Isaiah 62:12)*. *"Thou hast with thine arm redeemed thy people, the sons of Jacob and Joseph. Selah"* *(Psalm 77:15)*.

Webster's 1828 Dictionary defines *redeemed* as follows: "Ransomed; delivered from bondage, distress, penalty, liability, or from the possession of another, by paying an equivalent."

Redemption: The word *redemption* as used, for example, in Psalm 111:9 is root word #6304, which is *Ped-ooth'*, meaning distinction, also deliverance, division, redeem, redemption. *"He sent redemption unto his people: he hath commanded his covenant for ever: holy and reverend is his name"* (Psalm 111:9).

The word *redemption* as used in the New Testament is root word #629 in **Strong's Exhaustive Concordance.** #629, *ap-ol-oo'-tro-sis*, means ransom in full, riddance, or (spec) Christian salvation; deliverance, redemption. Another root word in the Greek which is related to #629 is #3083, *Loo'-tron*, something to loosen with, i.e, a redemption price, atonement): ransom.

The word *redemption* is defined in **Webster's 1828 Dictionary of the English Language** as follows: "6. In Theology, the purchase of God's favor by the death and sufferings of Christ; the ransom or deliverance of sinners from the bondage of sin and the penalties of God's violated law by the atonement of Christ. In whom we have redemption through his blood. Eph i. Col. i."

Salvation: The word *salvation* in **Strong's Exhaustive Concordance** as used in Isaiah 46:13 and Jeremiah 3:23, for example, is word #8668, *Tesh-oo-aw'*, meaning to rescue, deliverance, help, safety, salvation, victory.

"I bring near my righteousness; it shall not be far off, and my salvation shall not tarry: and I will place salvation in Zion for Israel my glory" (Isaiah 46:13). *"Truly in vain is salvation hoped for from the hills,*

and from the multitude of mountains: truly in the LORD our God is the salvation of Israel" (Jeremiah 3:23).

The word *salvation* as used in Luke 1:77 and 19:9, is #4991: This word #4991 appears as follows in **Strong's Exhaustive Concordance:** *So-tay-ree'-ah,* meaning to rescue or safety (physical or moral); deliver, health, salvation, save, saving.

"To give knowledge of salvation unto his people by the remission of their sins" (Luke 1:77). "And Jesus said unto him, This day is salvation come to this house, forsomuch as he also is a son of Abraham" (Luke 19:9).

The word *salvation* is defined as follows in **Webster's 1828 Dictionary of the English Language:** "Salvation, 1. The act of saving; preservation from destruction, danger or great calamity. 2. Appropriately in theology, the redemption of man from the bondage of sin and liability to eternal death, and the conferring on him everlasting happiness. This is the great salvation. Godly sorrow worketh repentance to salvation. 2 Cor. vii. 3. Deliverance from enemies; victory. Ex. xiv. 4. Remission of sins, or saving graces. Luke xix..."

From an **Expository Dictionary of New Testament Words, W. E. Vine:** Under Redeem Redemption: denotes to buy out...especially of purchasing a slave with a view to freedom...payment of a ransom. Under Salvation: Denotes deliverance, preservation, salvation. Salvation is used in the N. T. of material and temporal deliverance from danger and apprehension...of the spiritual and eternal deliverance granted immediately by God to those who accept His conditions of repentance and faith in the Lord Jesus, in whom alone it is to be obtained.

The two words *redemption* and *salvation* are sometimes confusing to Christian people. However, they are indeed explicit in meaning. Redeem or redemption is to buy back, to pay a ransom, to redeem. As used in the Holy Bible, redeem (redemption) has to do with the death of Jesus Christ in making the ransom for a people captive to sin (example Israel as in Exodus 15:13)) and thereby securing their redemption.

The word *salvation* means deliverance, preservation, safety, victory and health to those who have been redeemed. Redemption is the accomplished fact of Jesus Christ redeeming His people. Salvation is the conferring or appropriation of that redemption upon those to whom it was intended. In summary, God the Father in **election** predestinated those who would share in redemption. The act of redemption made by Jesus Christ upon the cross made the election of God the Father possible. God the Holy Spirit by His office and person confers this redemption upon the elect who receive salvation and are thereby saved, delivered, preserved, and made heirs of God's grace.

It is not possible to assert that redemption is for one people and salvation for another. Salvation is the appropriation of what was secured in redemption. You cannot have one without the other. There could be no salvation without the redemption secured by the death of Jesus Christ. You might deposit money in the bank (an accomplished fact), but if you never appropriated this money. it would remain on deposit and be unused by you. Redemption made it possible for God the Father to confer salvation upon those chosen in election. If that redemption was never appropriated, no one would ever be saved, for salvation would not be conferred. Salvation is the appropriation of the redemption secured by Jesus Christ in His suffering and death for His people.

With these definitions in mind, we are ready to build our presuppositions in the pages that follow. Gird up your spiritual loins and let God and Scripture alone determine what you believe about salvation. Do not trust your intellect, your will, or your emotions. They will fail you. Do not allow others to tell you what to believe. Believe God and Scripture. If you are ready to allow the Holy Spirit to guide you into a series of correct presuppositions on the subject of salvation, read on.

4

BUILDING BIBLE PRESUPPOSITIONS

For Whom Did Jesus Christ Die?

In the pages that follow, our goal is to build valid presuppositions that will establish the ground and foundation for building truth. Everyone has presuppositions from which various beliefs are built. What are your presuppositions regarding salvation? Are your premises built from human reason or Scripture? Have you gleaned them from studying the Bible or from reading and listening to information that others have passed along to you? The following presuppositions are general summaries based solely on the Bible. It may be necessary to study the Bible for years, reading it through several times a year, before you can really dig down to the bedrock of Bible truth. I pray that a fresh anointing of the Holy Spirit will be upon your life as you read these presuppositions, which are the result of careful and thoughtful reading and meditation of the Bible, Genesis to Revelation, over a period of forty-five years.

Presuppositions are those ideas or premises which are assumed beforehand. They are beliefs taken for granted in advance of a thing or a condition. What are the ideas you hold about salvation as we enter this study? Have you given careful examination to the presuppositions that you entertain about salvation? Can you be certain that your presuppositions are valid? Will they hold up to Bible truth? I pray that with a willing heart you will examine your presuppositions as the following positions are established from the Bible. Take each one of these premises and see if you can refute them from the Word of God. If you are unable to refute them from Scripture, you are left with no choice but to embrace them as your own.

THE GOD OF ABRAHAM, ISAAC, & JACOB

It may come as a surprise to many, but the God who wrote the Bible declares Himself to be the covenant God of one people. While God may be the Creator of the universe and all people on earth, He declares Himself to be a personal God to one people on the earth. Before you judge this statement, give yourself time to examine a number of Scriptures in the Bible. What does God say of Himself? Will you believe what God says?

When God appeared to Moses at the burning bush, He declared, *"...I am the God of thy father, the God of Abraham, the God of Isaac, and the God of Jacob. And Moses hid his face; for he was afraid to look upon God" (Exodus 3:6).* Again in Exodus 3:13-16 when God revealed His name to Moses, He declared Himself to be the God of Abraham, Isaac, and Jacob: *"And God said moreover unto Moses, Thus shalt thou say unto the children of Israel, the LORD God of your fathers, the God of Abraham, the God of Isaac, and the God of Jacob, hath sent me unto you:..."* Reading again in Exodus 3:16: *"Go, and gather the elders of Israel together, and say unto them, the LORD God of your fathers, the God of Abraham, of Isaac, and of Jacob, appeared unto me, saying, I have surely visited you,..."*

That the same God who wrote the Bible is particularly the God of Abraham, Isaac, and Jacob is a reoccurring theme throughout the Bible. Exodus 4:5 establishes again the importance of this fact. It was imperative that the children of Israel understand that the same God who had called Moses forth to deliver the Israelites from bondage was also the God of Abraham, Isaac, and Jacob. It is especially important to note that in Exodus 6:3, God reveals His personal covenant name to Israel, His people: *"And I appeared unto Abraham, unto Isaac, and unto Jacob, by the name of God Almighty, but by my name JEHOVAH was I not known to them."*

From this point forward the God of Abraham, Isaac, and *Jacob* would be the God of Abraham, Isaac, and *Israel.* Elijah confirmed this at Mt. Carmel when the false priests of Baal were being challenged by the God of Israel: *"And it came to pass at the time of the offering of the evening sacrifice, that Elijah the prophet came near, and said, Lord God of Abraham, Isaac, and of Israel, let it be known this day that thou art God in Israel,..." (I Kings 18:36).* In David's farewell blessing to His people He declared: *"O Lord God of Abraham, Isaac, and of Israel, our fathers, keep this for ever in the imagination of the thoughts of the heart of thy people..." (I Chronicles 29:18).* Hezekiah, the great King of Judah, made an appeal for the Israelites to keep the Passover by declaring to them: *"So the posts went with the letters from the king and his princes throughout all Israel and Judah, and according to the commandment of the king, saying, Ye children of Israel, turn again unto the Lord God of Abraham, Isaac, and Israel, and he will return to the remnant of you..." (II Chronicles 30:6).*

This special theme is not lost in the New Testament. In Matthew 22:32, Mark 12:26, and Luke 20:37, reference is made to God being the God of Abraham, Isaac, and Jacob. In speaking of the resurrection to come, Jesus Christ declared in Matthew 22:32: *"I am the God of Abraham, and the God of Isaac, and the God of Jacob? God is not the God of the dead, but of the living."* In Luke 20:37, Jesus Christ drew attention to the fact that at the burning bush God had declared Himself to be the God of Abraham, Isaac, and Jacob. *"Now that the dead are raised, even Moses shewed at the bush, when he calleth the LORD the God of Abraham, and the God of Isaac, and the God of Jacob."* The apostles carried this theme forward in their ministry, as evidenced in the life of Peter (Acts 3:13): *"The God of Abraham, and of Isaac, and of Jacob, the God of our fathers, hath glorified his son Jesus;..."* Again in Acts 7:32, Stephen calls attention to the fact that the God of Scripture revealed Himself to be the God of Abraham, Isaac, and Jacob at the burning bush.

By what *authority* do Christians believe the God of the Bible to be the God who has embraced all the world in salvation? Most certainly, the God of the Bible is the God of all creation. Furthermore, this God can be known and worshipped by all the creation. But in terms of His becoming a personal God in covenant relationship, He is the God of Abraham, Isaac, and Israel only. It would be ridiculous for someone to proclaim that **Allah**, the god of the Moslems, was God of all the earth. Allah is the god that is revered and worshipped by the Moslems. Neither would it be acceptable to call **Brahman**, the god of the Hindus, the God of all people. In similar fashion, it is not appropriate and simply inaccurate to call the God of the Bible, **JEHOVAH,** the God of any people but Abraham, Isaac, and Jacob Israel. Do you believe the Bible? Do you believe that God is the God of Abraham, Isaac, and Israel? Do you believe that the God of Scripture extends salvation to all people, races, and nations on earth? Can the God who declared Himself to be the God of Abraham, Isaac, and Israel be called the God of all? Thank you for allowing the Bible to answer the question *do all races share in salvation?*

THE BIBLE IS THE BOOK OF ADAM'S RACE

The Bible declares itself to be the book of one people on earth: *"This is the book of the generations of Adam. In the day that God created man, in the likeness of God made he him; Male and female created he them; and blessed them, and called their name Adam, in the day when they were created"* (Genesis 5:1-2). The Bible does not claim to be the book for any people other than Adam and his seed. Only the **chronology** of Adam's children is in the Bible. Specifically, you will find a detailed chronology only for the seed of Abraham, Isaac, and Jacob-Israel in the Bible. The genealogies of the Mongoloid and Negroid are not there. This does not mean that God did not create these races. It simply means that the Bible is not intended for any people other than those to whom it is written.

God revealed Himself by special revelation to the children of Abraham, Isaac, and Jacob-Israel: *"The secret things belong unto the LORD our God: but those things which are revealed belong unto us and to our children for ever, that we may do all the words of this law"* (Deuteronomy 29:29). The Bible is a special revelation that is exclusive to the generations of Adam, Enos, Cainan, Mahalaleel, Jared, Enoch, Methuselah, Lamech, Noah, Shem, Arphaxad, Salah, Eber, Peleg, Reu, Serug, Nahor, Terah, Abraham, Isaac, Jacob, the twelve tribes descending from Jacob's sons, and the vast millions descended from them. That the God of the Bible revealed His law only to these people is confirmed in Psalm 147:19-20: *"He sheweth his word unto Jacob, his statutes and his judgments unto*

Israel. He hath not dealt so with any nation: and as for his judgments, they have not known them. Praise ye the LORD.*"*

The God who wrote the Bible said this about His people Israel: *"...O children of Israel, against the whole family which I brought up from the land of Egypt, saying, You only have I known of all the families of the earth: therefore I will punish you for all your iniquities"* (Amos 3:1-2). God declared Himself to be the God of only one people. Must we reinvent or rewrite the Bible to allow a belief that salvation extends to all races? Since the Bible is not the family history of any people but the race of Adam, primarily the seed of Abraham, Isaac, and Jacob-Israel within Adam, can we universalize the Bible to be the book for all people of the earth? What God has ordained, let no man change.

Please examine your presuppositions about the Bible. Who is the Bible written to, for, and about? Can the family history of one people suddenly become the family history of every other race? What if your neighbors, unrelated to you by blood or kinship, suddenly claimed your family history. In a court of law, would they be able to defend themselves as being heirs of any wealth accruing to you from a deceased relative? By what Scriptural authority can all the races of the earth become heirs to that which God promised only to the seed of Abraham, Isaac, and Jacob Israel? Can the God of the Bible be the Savior of all races on earth? **Is There Salvation for All Races?**

THERE IS NO RACIAL UNITY IN ADAM

People commonly assume that Adam and Eve are the parents and progenitors of all races on earth. Moreover, clergy all over the world are guilty of preaching this. They simply assume that all races on planet had their beginning with Adam. This presupposition undergirds most theological rationale. In the post Genesis flood, they assume that the three sons of Noah--Shem, Ham, and Japheth-- are the progenitors of the racial differences on the earth today. Ham is most often considered to be the progenitor of the Negroid race, while the Mongoloids descended from Japheth and the Caucasoids from Shem. In both pre-flood and post-flood history, most clergy and millions of Christian laymen have all races of the earth descending from Adam (pre-flood) and Noah (post-flood).

The Bible does not teach that all races originated in Adam. Such a notion is evolution! This is a theory right out of the heart of evolutionary humanism. If you believe that the Mongoloid, Negroid, and Caucasoid races are all descended from one man (Adam) and one woman (Eve), you may call yourself a believer in evolution, regardless of your church affiliation. The Bible is emphatic! Adam is the father of only one race. The Hebrew derivation and meaning of the word *Adam* links it exclusively to the Caucasoid race. A careful examination of the word *man* (Genesis 1:26) in Genesis 2:7 and Genesis 5:1 confirms that it is root word #120 in **Strong's Exhaustive Concordance to the Bible.** Root word #120 is *Aw-Dawm'*, from #119, ruddy, i.e., a human being (an individual or the species, mankind, etc) man, person. Root word #119 is *Aw-Dam'*, to show blood in the face, flush or turn rose, be (dyed, made) red (ruddy). All pure Caucasians are Adamites. The Caucasian race is the race of Adam man.

The only way that a person can build a unity of all races is to set aside the plain teaching of the Bible and adopt the position of evolutionary humanism. Since all races do not share a unity in Adam, they do not share the lineage, heritage, and family history of the Adamic race. **Every race has its own particular heritage and family history.** To say that the history, lineage, and heritage of Adam kind have nothing in common with the Negroid or Mongoloid races is certainly not prejudiced, even though today's society might say otherwise. All races have their own particular destiny and purpose to fulfill in the plan of the Creator. What was planned for Adam kind was not what the Creator purposed for the Mongoloid and Negroid races. **Unity of all races does not pass the test of Biblical scholarship.** Hence, there is no foundation for the idea that salvation extends to all races.

ORIGINAL SIN ONLY IN ADAM KIND

The notion of salvation for all races breaks down completely when the false presupposition that all races originated in Adam is removed. Furthermore, if all races did not descend from Adam, all races cannot share in the original sin gained at the fall. The Bible teaches that in Adam, we sinned all. *"Wherefore, as by one man sin entered into the world, and death by sin; and so death passed upon all men, for that all have sinned"* (Romans 5:12). Death passed unto Adam and all of his descendants. The Creator kept His promise to Adam as in Genesis 2:17: *"But of the tree of the knowledge of good and evil, thou shalt not eat of it: for in the day that thou eatest thereof thou shalt surely die."* The ground and foundation for the need of a savior is predicated on the fact that we all sinned with Adam. If you believe in original sin, birth sin, and that death passed upon all of Adam's descendants, you are in proper accord with the truth of Christianity.

All of Adam's descendants came under the law of sin and death. Every man and woman born into this world of Adam's race are born with birth (original) sin. *Children do not acquire sin; they are born with sin.* Sin is inherited from the fall! Only Adam's descendants are born into sin and death, and therefore, only Adam's descendants must be delivered, saved from the law of sin and death. Hence, salvation is inseparably linked to the fall of Adam. Races not descended from Adam are not born into sin. Adam was the only race placed under law at creation (Genesis 2:17). Original (birth) sin is chargeable only to Adam and his descendants. The other non-Adamic races are not under the liability of sin. The responsibility for obedience to the Creator's law fell upon Adam. Hence, breaking that law had awesome consequences for Adam and all of his descendants. How can one claim salvation for all races if all races are not included in Adam's sin? If the curse and penalty for disobedience fell only upon Adam kind, the other races do not share in Adam's liability. The very need for salvation for the non-Adamic races becomes unnecessary.

ALL RACES WERE NOT UNDER LAW

Only Adam and his descendants transgressed the law; hence, they alone need salvation. Romans 5:13 declares that *"...sin is not imputed when there is no law."* We read in Romans 4:15: *"...for where no law is, there is no transgression."* In Romans 3:20 the Scripture makes clear that *"...by the law is the knowledge of sin."* Without the law there is no knowledge of sin. I John 3:4 reads: *"Whosoever committeth sin transgresseth also the law; for sin is the transgression of the law."* In the beginning God gave the dominion of the earth to Adamic creation (Genesis 1:28, 2:15-17, and 3:17-19). The law was the means by which **dominion of the earth** would be achieved. The liability to know, understand, and walk in obedience to the law belonged to Adam, not the other races.

The non-Adamic races were never under law. They did not participate in the fall of Adam into sin, so they are under no liability in the transgression of the law. Sin is not imputed unto them, and they have no need for salvation. The curse of the law passed only to Adam and his descendants. Hence, the need for the saving grace of Jesus Christ is only for those under the curse (penalty), which was death.

Remember that the dominion mandate required that Adam be under law and accountable to His Creator (Genesis 1:28 and 2:15). The non-Adamic races were not charged with the dominion and were not placed under law. They did not need to be saved because they were not under the curse of the law. **Salvation is for those who were under the penalty of the law.** All of the non-Adamic races remain as they were before the fall. Their highest and most noble attainment in this world is to fulfill that mission or destiny designed by their Creator God. To impute the sin of Adam to all the other races is pure folly. We dare not change what God ordained. Think again if you believe that salvation is for all races. If you want to build from the truth of God's Word, begin with the presupposition that salvation is not for all races.

THE ELECTION OF GOD THE FATHER

The Holy Scriptures emphatically teach that there is an **election** of God the Father which was purposed in the divine counsel of His own will before the world began. The Bible is a record of how God the Father purposed to save a people of his own choosing (election). It sets forth the means by which election would be made possible (in the redemption of Jesus Christ) and how He effectually calls these people into a living faith by the power of the Holy Ghost. Moreover, the Bible loudly proclaims the people whom the Father elected. This election begins in **Adam, Seth, Enos, Cainan, Mahalaleel, Jared, Enoch, Methuselah, Lamech, and Noah** (pre-flood history--Genesis 5) and continues with **Shem, Arphaxad, Salah, Eber, Peleg, Reu,**

Serug, Nahor, Terah, Abraham, Isaac, Jacob, the twelve tribes (post flood history) **and the millions** (Genesis 15:5, 24:60) descending from them.

Scripture pointedly identifies the covenant lineage of Adam to Noah and Shem to Abraham, Isaac, and Jacob-Israel to be the elect of God the Father. There is not a verse in the Bible indicating that God annulled this elect covenant or in some manner admitted defeat in His purpose to save a particular people. Indeed, the Bible confirms that one of the virtues of JEHOVAH'S character is that His Word is unchangeable. God cannot lie (Titus 1:2, Hebrews 6:18), and He will not alter His Word (Malachi 3:6, Psalm 33:11, Hebrews 13:8, Psalm 111:7,8). What God the Father purposed to do in election (Ephesians 1:4-5), He did by the good pleasure which He purposed in Himself and worked out in the counsel of his own will (Ephesians 1:9-11). God the Father did not choose His elect because they were good or deserving, because He could foresee their faith in the Lord Jesus Christ, or because they were superior to any other people.

In fact, it is imperative to note that *God the Father was under obligation to save no one!* However, we all sinned in Adam (Romans 3:23, 5:12, Ecclesiastes 7:20, Psalm 14:2-3, 51:5, 53:2-3). In the beginning (Genesis 2:15-17), God put a hedge about Adam and commanded him to not eat of the fruit of the tree of knowledge of good and evil. Adam was created with a **bias to do only good**; he did not possess sin nature, but the *possibility* to sin. **He knew no evil.** When Adam sinned against God by transgressing the law, he and all of his descendants came under the **law of sin and death** (Romans 8:1-2). In the fall, Adam and all of his descendants became estranged from God the Father, lost in sin, and a slave to sin and death. The spirit (pneuma) was made passive toward God, the soul (psyche) became depraved, and the body (soma) was given over to passion and lust of the flesh. In this condition, God the Father was under liability to save no one.

God elected us out of His own divine purpose, for His own good pleasure, and in terms of His own sovereign will. In response to so great an election, St. Paul could say: *"What shall we then say to these things? If God be for us, who can be against us?...Who shall lay any thing to the charge of God's elect? It is God that justifieth"* (Romans 8:31,33). Because God the Father chose a certain people and passed others by, can we say that God is unrighteous? What saith the Scripture? *"What shall we say then? Is there unrighteousness with God? God forbid. For he saith to Moses, I will have mercy on whom I will have mercy, and I will have compassion on whom I will have compassion"* (Romans 9:14-15). Consider also Romans 9:21: *"Hath not the potter power over the clay, of the same lump to make one vessel unto honour, and another unto dishonour?"*

One need not look very far into the Holy Scriptures to identify the people whom God chose in election. Beginning with Adam, God the Father purposed to rescue and save an elect group of people in every generation. Included in this group would be a lineage of people from Adam to Noah (pre-flood) and from Shem to Abraham, Isaac, Jacob-Israel and the twelve tribes (post-flood). The following Scriptures are just a few of the multitude of Bible citations that can be marshalled to demonstrate who is chosen of God the Father in Scripture, time, and history.

Genesis 17:7 says, **"And I will establish my covenant between me and thee and thy seed after thee in their generations for an everlasting covenant, to be a God unto thee, and to thy seed after thee."**

Genesis 17:19: *"And God said, Sarah thy wife shall bear thee a son indeed; and thou shalt call his name Isaac: and I will establish my covenant with him for an everlasting covenant, and with his seed after him."*

Genesis 24:60: *"And they blessed Rebekah, and said unto her, Thou art our sister, be thou the mother of thousands of millions, and let thy seed possess the gate of those which hate them."*

Genesis 35:11: *"And God said unto him, (Jacob-Israel), I am God Almighty: be fruitful and multiply; a nation and a company of nations shall be of thee, and kings shall come out of thy loins;"*

Genesis 48:16: *"The Angel which redeemed me from all evil, bless the lads; and let my name be named on them, and the name of my fathers Abraham and Isaac; and let them grow into a multitude in the midst of the earth."*

Exodus 3:24: *"And God heard their groaning, and God remembered his covenant with Abraham, with Isaac, and with Jacob."*

Exodus 15:13,16: *"Thou in thy mercy hast led forth the people which thou hast redeemed:....Fear and dread shall fall upon them; by the greatness of thine arm...till the people pass over, which thou hast purchased."*

Leviticus 26:42: *"Then will I remember my covenant with Jacob, and also my covenant with Isaac, and also my covenant with Abraham will I remember;..."*

Numbers: 24:2,5: *"And Balaam lifted up his eyes, and he saw Israel abiding in his tents according to their tribes; and the spirit of God came upon him,...How goodly are thy tents, O Jacob, and thy tabernacles, O Israel!"*

Deuteronomy 7:6: *"For thou (Israel) art an holy people unto the LORD thy God: the LORD thy God hath chosen thee to be a special people unto himself, above all people that are upon the face of the earth."*

Deuteronomy 14:2: *"For thou art an holy people unto the LORD thy God, and the LORD hath chosen thee to be a peculiar people unto himself, above all the nations that are upon the earth."*

Deuteronomy 32:8-9: *"When the Most High divided to the nations their inheritance, when he separated the sons of Adam, he set the bounds of the people according to the number of the children of Israel. For the LORD's portion is his people; Jacob is the lot of his inheritance."*

II Samuel 7:23-24: *"And what one nation in the earth is like thy people, even like Israel, whom God went to redeem for a people to himself, and to make him a name, and to do for you great things...For thou hast confirmed to thyself thy people Israel to be a people unto thee for ever: and thou, LORD, art become their God."*

Psalms 135:4: *"For Yahweh hath chosen Jacob unto himself, and Israel for his peculiar treasure."*

Isaiah 41:8: *"But thou, Israel, art my servant, Jacob whom I have chosen, the seed of Abraham my friend."*

Isaiah 43:21: *"This people (Israel) have I formed for myself; they shall shew forth my praise."*

Isaiah 44:1-2: *"Yet now hear, O Jacob my servant; and Israel, whom I have chosen: Thus saith the LORD that made thee, and formed thee from the womb, which will help thee; Fear not, O Jacob my servant;..."*

Isaiah 45:4: *"For Jacob my servant's sake, and Israel mine elect, I have even called thee by thy name: I have surnamed thee, though thou hast not known me."*

Isaiah 45:17,25: *"But Israel shall be saved in the LORD with an everlasting salvation: ye shall not be ashamed nor confounded world without end....In the LORD shall all the seed of Israel be justified, and shall glory."*

Jeremiah 31:1,3: *"At the same time, saith the LORD, will I be the God of all the families of Israel, and they shall be my people...I have loved thee with an everlasting love: therefore with lovingkindness have I drawn thee."*

Jeremiah 31:31,33: *"Behold, the days come, saith the LORD, that I will make a new covenant with the house of Israel, and with the house of Judah:...But this shall be the covenant that I will make with the house of Israel; After those days, saith the LORD, I will put my law in their inward parts, and write it in their hearts; and will be their God, and they shall be my people."*

Amos 3:1-2: *"...O children of Israel, against the whole family which I brought up from the land of Egypt, saying, You only have I known of all the families of the earth: therefore I will punish you for all your iniquities."*

Matthew 1:21: *"And she shall bring forth a son, and thou shalt call his name JESUS: for he shall save his people from their sins."*

Matthew 10:5-6: *"These twelve Jesus sent forth, and commanded them, saying, Go not into the way of the Gentiles,...But go rather to the lost sheep of the house of Israel."*

Matthew 15:24: *"But he answered and said, I am not sent but unto the lost sheep of the house of Israel."*

Matthew 19:28: *"...Verily I say unto you, That ye which have followed me, in the regeneration when the Son of man shall sit in the throne of his glory, ye also shall sit upon twelve thrones, judging the twelve tribes of Israel."*

Luke 1:32-33: *"He shall be great, and shall be called the Son of the Highest: and the LORD God shall give unto him the throne of his father David: And he shall reign over the house of Jacob for ever; and of his kingdom there shall be no end."*

Luke 1:68,72: *"Blessed be the LORD God of Israel; for he hath visited and redeemed his people,...To perform the mercy promised to our fathers, and to remember his holy covenant."*

Luke 24:21: *"But we trusted that it had been he which should have redeemed Israel: ..."*

Acts 5:31: *"Him hath God exalted with his right hand to be a Prince and a Saviour, for to give repentance to Israel, and forgiveness of sins."*

Acts 13:23: *"Of this man's seed hath God according to his promise raised unto Israel a Saviour, Jesus:"*

Acts 26:6-7: *"And now I stand an judged for the hope of the promise made of God unto our fathers: Unto which promise our twelve tribes, instantly serving God day and night, hope to come..."*

Romans 9:4-5: *"Who are Israelites; to whom pertaineth the adoption, and the glory, and the covenants, and the giving of the law, and the service of God, and the promises; Whose are the fathers, and of whom as concerning the flesh Christ came, who is over all, God blessed for ever. Amen."*

Romans 10:1: *"Brethren, my heart's desire and prayer to God for Israel is, that they might be saved."*

Romans 11:2,5: *"God hath not cast away his people which he foreknew...Even so then at this present time also there is a remnant according to the election of grace."*

I Corinthians 10:1: *"Moreover, brethren, I would not that ye should be ignorant, how that all our fathers were under the cloud, and all passed through the sea."*

Galatians 6:16: *"And as many as walk according to this rule, peace be on them, and mercy, and upon the Israel of God."*

Hebrews 8:10: *"For this is the covenant that I will make with the house of Israel after those days, saith the Lord; I will put my laws into their mind, and write them in their hearts; and I will be to them a God, and they shall be to me a people."*

James 1:1: *"James, a servant of God and of the Lord Jesus Christ, to the twelve tribes which are scattered abroad, greeting."*

I Peter 1:1-2: *"Peter, an apostle of Jesus Christ, to the strangers...Elect according to the foreknowledge of God the Father, through sanctification of the Spirit, unto obedience and sprinkling of the blood of Jesus Christ: Grace unto you, and peace, be multiplied."*

Revelation 21:9,12: *"...Come hither, I will shew thee the bride, the Lamb's wife...And had a wall great and high, and had twelve gates, and at the gates twelve angels, and names written thereon, which are the names of the twelve tribes of the children of Israel:"*

This wealth of Scripture testifies to an elect people chosen by God the Father to be heirs of salvation. The story of this **election of a people to salvation** is the real message of the Bible. The Bible reserves the election for the covenant lineage that begins with Adam and extends through

Israel and the twelve tribes. The election of God does not allow for the salvation of all races. Such a theory requires that a whole new Bible be written.

THE ADOPTION BELONGS TO DIVORCED ISRAEL

Those who contend for a Gospel that embraces all races in salvation are always ready to adopt the other races into the election of God. They concede that there is an election. However, then they proceed to defend a position of adoption whereby God, in mercy, grafts members of every race into the Israel of God. Indeed, this **adoption** is carried in theology to a point where the people of the adoption become the new Israel (modern church), and literal Israel, the people of the genuine election, become lost in history. Is man playing God? Today, the primary body of believers in the Christian world are considered *Gentiles* who are *adopted* into the root stock of literal Israel.

The adoption spoken of in the Bible belongs to literal Israel. Examine the following Scriptures: *"Who are Israelites; to whom pertaineth the adoption, and the glory, and the covenants, and the giving of the law, and the service of God, and the promises" (Romans 9:4)*. Note in this verse that the adoption pertains to Israel. *"But when the fulness of the time was come, God sent forth his Son, made of a woman, made under the law, To redeem them that were under the law, that we might receive the adoption of sons" (Galatians 4:4-5)*. Again, Israel, the people under Law, are the ones to whom pertaineth the adoption in Galatians 4:4-5. This truth is confirmed in Ephesians 1:4-5 where the adoption, referenced here, is to Israel, the people chosen in Christ before the foundation of the world. *"According as he hath chosen us in him before the foundation of the world, that we should be holy and without blame before him in love: Having predestinated us unto the adoption of children by Jesus Christ to himself, according to the good pleasure of his will."*

In every case where the word *adoption* is used in the New Testament, it comes from a Greek root word #5206, *huiothesia*, from a presumed comp. of 5207 and a der. of 5087; the placing as a son, i.e. adoption (fig. Chr. sonship in respect to God): adoption (of children, of sons). See **Strong's Exhaustive Concordance to the Bible.** Adoption in Scripture refers specifically to that branch of the House of Israel (ten-tribed Israel) who was divorced (Jeremiah 3:8, Isaiah 50:1, Isaiah 54:1, Hosea 1:4) and carried into dispersion among the nations. At the death of Solomon in B. C. 975, the House of Israel was divided into two separate kingdoms: Judah and Israel. Israel of the Northern Kingdom was made up of ten tribes. After a period of more than two hundred and fifty years of idolatry and breaking covenant with *Jehovah*, these people, as many as ten million of them, were carried away by the Assyrian kings (I Kings 18:11) and placed in the vast lands of the Medes and Persians. Here they multiplied and expanded to fill up all of Asia Minor. They migrated north from the Caucasus into Northern and Western Europe, the British Isles, and on to the far north and western regions of the Western Hemisphere.

These vast millions of people, ready receivers of the Gospel of Jesus Christ, were the people who were adopted into the truth of Christianity. In the New Testament they are called Gentiles. These New Testament Gentiles, a non-people, were the long, lost Israelites who had been divorced by their God, sent into dispersion among the nations, and filled the landscape of most of the Greek speaking world by the first century of the Christian era. These were the people who received the attention of St. Paul and were the subjects of his epistles. Indeed, in his letter to the Ephesians, Paul had this to say about the Gentiles, or ten-tribed Israel that had been divorced and cast away: *"That at that time ye were without Christ, being aliens from the commonwealth of Israel, and strangers from the covenants of promise, having no hope, and without God in the world:"* (*Ephesians 2:12*).

Most assuredly, the adoption did pertain to Israel in dispersion, and not to any other people. The **wild olive branch** of Romans 11 fame is none other than Israel in dispersion. The Gentiles spoken of by St. Paul in Romans 11:13 were **Israel in dispersion** who were becoming ready hearers of the Word of God. Final proof for the wild olive branch of Romans 11 being literal Israel is found in Romans 11:26 where St. Paul makes the declaration: *"...all Israel shall be saved..."* He refers to the fact that the House of Israel, divorced and scattered among the nations, will be grafted in, *adopted*, into the **natural olive** (the House of Judah that had never been divorced). The Old Testament ends with the House of Israel divided into separate and sovereign kingdoms and with the promise of **reunification, regathering, and restoration.** Lost Israel in dispersion among the nations really was *not* lost. They were called forth in the fullness of time by a sovereign God and adopted back into the natural olive (Romans 11). That middle wall of partition (Ephesians 2:14) between **Israel and Judah** had been broken down by Jesus Christ and His sacrifice upon the cross.

Those who trust in the theology of adoption as a means of getting all races into God's plan of salvation will come up with empty buckets from the living Word of God. The well of salvation water can only quench the thirst of those who are in the election of God. Israel in dispersion, millions of them, are the people who have historically embraced Christianity, printed Bibles, and established churches throughout the western culture. Salvation for all races may be a popular religious dogma, but it cannot be defended from the Word of God. The adoption never applied to any people other than literal Israel, dispersed among the nations. The justified heathen (Galatians 3:8), the Barbarian, Scythians (Colossians 3:11), and the Greeks (Romans 1:14, I Corinthians 1:22) were all **literal Israel**, estranged from their God, in exile from the covenants of promise (Ephesians 2:12), but surely known to God the Father and Jesus Christ His Son.

THE GENTILES ARE LITERAL ISRAEL

Those who advocate the salvation for all races often resort to the Gentiles as their strongest defense for including all races in the Gospel. *Most clergy believe that the Gentiles encompass every race, nation, and people outside of **literal and physical Israel**.* That the Gentiles of the New Testament could be the House of Israel, divorced and sent into dispersion, is a thought most clergy and their followers have not entertained. Usually, taking the Gospel to the Gentiles is viewed as going to every race that does not include what most Christians call the **Jews.** They view the word *Jew* as a synonym for the word *Israel*. Because the Gentiles of the New Testament are generally considered to include any people other than Biblical Israel, a few appropriate comments will now be in order.

A brief discussion on the meaning of the word *Gentile* will be helpful. **Webster's 1828 Dictionary of the English Language** defines Gentile as follows: **"Gentile, n...From L. gens, nation, race; applied to pagans. In the scriptures, a pagan; a worshipper of false gods; any person not a Jew or a christian; a heathen. The Hebrews included in the term goim or nations, all the** tribes of men who had not received the true faith, and were not circumcised. The christians translated goim by the L. gentes, and imitated the Jews in giving the name gentiles to all nations who were not Jews nor christians. In civil affairs, the denomination was given to all nations who were not Romans."

The Random House Dictionary of the English Language defines *Gentile* in the following manner: "1. of or pertaining to any people not Jewish. 2. Christian, as distinguished from Jewish. 3. Mormonism, neither Mormon nor Jewish. 4. heathen or pagan. 5. (of a linguistic expression) expressing nationality or local origins. 6. of or pertaining to a tribe, clan, people, nation, etc. 7. a person who is not Jewish, esp. a Christian. 8. (among Mormons) a person who is not a Mormon. 9. a heathen or pagan. Also, Gentile."

Strong's Exhaustive Concordance to the Bible defines the word *Gentile* as follows: In the Old Testament the Hebrew root word translated *Gentile* is #1471, *goy*: **foreign nation; hence a Gentile; also (fig.) a troop of animals, or a flight of Locusts; Gentile, heathen, nation, people.** In the New Testament the Greek root word translated *Gentile* is #1484, **Ethnos, a race (as of the same habit) i.e. a tribe; spec. a foreign (non-Jewish) one (usually by impl. pagan): Gentile, heathen, nation, people.**

The dictionary definitions confirm that the word *Gentile* has broad interpretations. In the Old Testament the word *Gentile* is the equivalent of heathen, nation, or people. In the New Testament, *Gentile* is the equivalent to heathen, nation, or people. It means essentially the same thing in both the Old and New Testaments.

In Genesis 17:5-6, the Bible declares: *"Neither shall thy name any more be called Abram, but thy name shall be*

Abraham; for a father of many nations have I made thee. And I will make thee exceeding fruitful, and I will make nations of thee, and kings shall come out of thee." Note that the word *nations* in the forgoing Scriptures are all from the Hebrew root word #1471 (**Strong's Exhaustive Concordance**), and mean gentile, heathen, nation, or people. If this word #1471 had been translated *Gentiles* as in Genesis 10:5, Abraham would have become known as the man who would be the father of many *Gentiles*. This being true, *Gentiles* in the New Testament would have been linked immediately to the literal seed of Abraham, Isaac, and Jacob-Israel. Indeed, Abraham did become the father of many nations (Genesis 35:11, Genesis 48:16,19); it is from these *nations* that the so-called *Gentiles* of the New Testament come.

Recall that when Israel was in spiritual apostasy in the Sinai Wilderness, about B. C. 1451, God gave a word through His servant Moses in which He declared: *"They (speaking of His people Israel) have moved me to jealousy with that which is not God: they have provoked me to anger with their vanities: and I will move them to jealousy with those which are not a people; I will provoke them to anger with a foolish nation"* (Deuteronomy 32:21). This prophesy has to do with the fact that Israel of the Northern Kingdom was to one day be divorced and sent into dispersion among the nations. In this state of divorce and estrangement, they would become the people scattered, as in Jezreel, not pitied as in Loruhamah, and not a people as in Loammi (Hosea 1). Divorced Israel was to no longer be God's people (Hosea 1:10). **They would become the people that were not a people, Gentiles, a non-people of history.** It is in this sense that St. Paul in Romans 10:19 is referencing Deuteronomy 32:21: *"But I say, Did not Israel know? first Moses saith, I will provoke you to jeal-*

*ousy by them that are no people, and by a foolish nation
I will anger you.*" Paul is now letting the House of Judah
know that Israel in dispersion, the people that are not a
people, will come to the saving knowledge of Jesus Christ
and will be used of God to provoke the House of Judah to
come to the knowledge of their God. Hence, St. Paul could
say in Romans 11:13-14: *"For I speak to you Gentiles,
(Israel in divorce and dispersion), inasmuch as I am the
apostle of the Gentiles, I magnify mine office: If by any
means I may provoke to emulation them which are my
flesh, and might save some of them."* St. Paul was of the
tribe of Benjamin (Romans 11:1); he was by religious tradi-
tion a Pharisee (Philippians 3:5) and a Jew (Acts 21:39,
22:3) by virtue of being born of those Israelites who were
considered part of the House of Judah. Having grown up in
the traditions of his father, Paul, a strict Pharisee who attended the school of Gamaliel (Acts 22:3), was raised to
look with disdain and contempt upon the Israelites of the
Northern Kingdom, who were considered barbarian, heathen, uncircumcised, and a people not a people, indeed
Gentiles. It was by the conversion of these people who were
not a people (Hosea 1:10) that Paul was provoking Israel of
the House of Judah (Deuteronomy 32:21, Romans 10:19,
and Romans 11:13-14) to come to the knowledge of the
Lord and Savior Jesus Christ.

It is important that the word *Gentiles* not be used as a
euphemism to soften or cushion the identification of the
people in the New Testament who are indeed the heathen,
barbarian, Greeks who were the divorced branch of the
House of Israel in dispersion among the nations. Indeed,
the Gentiles of the New Testament are literal physical Israel, the people who are not a people (Hosea 1:10), but were
to become the people of the living God (Hosea 2:23). For
this reason, St. Paul could declare that these Gentiles (Ro-

mans 2:14,15) were by nature doing things contained in the law, thus showing the work of the law written in their hearts. (This is a confirmation of Jeremiah 31:31-33--that the new covenant would be written in the heart of the House of Israel by the effectual power of the Holy Spirit.) Paul could thus say of the Gentiles, *"Which shew the work of the law written in their hearts, their conscience also bearing witness, and their thoughts the mean while accusing or else excusing one another:)"* (Romans 2:15).

A great turning point in the history of early Christianity came with the Gospel being taken to the Gentiles. Acts 10 and the conversion of **Cornelius,** a man considered a Gentile, was a watershed event in the history of the Church. Cornelius was a genetic Israelite, a member of the divorced nation of Israel then in dispersion. He, being considered outside the commonwealth of Israel (Ephesians 2:12), would have been considered a Gentile, a barbarian, a heathen, unfit to share in the community of the early Christians (who were converts from the Kingdom of Judah) and in the new found faith that they had in Jesus Christ. When the apostle Peter was sent by the Holy Spirit to bring the good news of the Gospel to Cornelius and his household, this occasioned a tremendous spiritual shock wave through the church. Indeed, Acts 11:18 records the reaction of the early Church upon hearing the revelation of God to the Gentiles: *"When they heard these things, they held their peace, and glorified God, saying, Then hath God also to the Gentiles granted repentance unto life"* (Acts 11:18). The opening of the door to the Gentiles was more than a mere introduction of Christianity to heathen unbelievers. It was the very fulfillment of Hosea 1:10. The non-people of divorced Israel, the people who were not a people (Gentiles), were at long last coming back to the knowledge of their God and His plan for their salvation.

Careful study of the Bible will close the door marked *Gentiles* to being used as a method of including all races in salvation. **Since the Gentiles are actually literal Israel in dispersion, there is no Scriptural authority for using the word *Gentile* as a term to bring all races into Christianity.** Let God be God, and let His Word be true. What God has elected to do in the sovereign counsel of His own will, let not man put asunder. The word Gentile as used in Scripture will not open the door for salvation to all races. That door is closed by authority of God and His Word. **The Gentile converts of the New Testament are genetic Israelites of the dispersion (dispora).**

5

THE LAW OF KINSMAN REDEEMER

A long forgotten law in Scripture that has direct implications on salvation is the **Law of Kinsman Redeemer.**
Any attempt to extend salvation to all races violates this
law, for **God does not break His own law!** A review of this
law as set forth in Leviticus 25:47-55 is imperative. Without
knowledge of this law, people may place the saving grace
of Jesus Christ outside the limits imposed by the Law of
Kinsman Redeemer.

*"And if a sojourner or stranger wax rich by thee, and
thy brother that dwelleth by him wax poor, and sell himself unto the stranger or sojourner by thee, or to the stock
of the stranger's family: After that he is sold he may be
redeemed again; one of his brethren may redeem him:
Either his uncle, or his uncle's son, may redeem him, or
any that is nigh of kin unto him of his family may redeem him; or if he be able, he may redeem himself"*
(Leviticus 25:47-49).

Please reflect for a moment upon this important law. It
was not uncommon in ancient Israel for a man to sell himself into the status of a bondservant to rectify unfortunate
circumstances in his life. After being sold into bondage, he
could redeem himself from that condition if his financial

circumstances changed and allowed him to. Any other near kinsman could also redeem him. A stranger or someone not related by blood could not redeem a bond servant from his condition of slavery. Instead, the right of redemption was granted to the person who was of the nearest kinship to the bond servant. This principle has full application in the case of Ruth. When the nearest kinsman refused the right of redemption for both the property and the woman (Ruth), the right of redemption passed to Boaz, the next nearest of kin to Ruth's husband.

In the matter of salvation, this Law of Kinsman Redemption has great significance. Recall that in Adam we all sinned. Scripture places every member of Adam's race under original (birth) sin. By sin, death entered into the world (Romans 5:12) and passed upon all men. **No member of Adam's race can escape the penalty of sin and death.** Adam and all his descendants were without a means of redeeming themselves from the bondage of sin and death. They needed a **near kinsman** to redeem them from this bondage. Since God required a firstborn male without blemish (spot or sin), no human qualified. Indeed, if any mortal *could* have qualified to be the sacrifice, surely it would have been Isaac when God commanded Abraham to offer him upon the altar (Genesis 22).

God the Father, acting for and on behalf of those people whom He had chosen in election before the foundation of the world (Ephesians 1:4-5), initiated a plan for the salvation of Israel. **Through the miraculous incarnation, Jesus Christ came in the role of a kinsman redeemer to save His people from their sin.** God transcended time and the universe to take upon Himself the seed of Abraham. The flesh body that Jesus Christ assumed in the incarnation was not just any kind of flesh. Jesus Christ came in the role of a kinsman redeemer. ***"For verily he took not on him the*** *nature of angels; but he took on him the seed of Abraham"* *(Hebrews 2:16)*. Why did Jesus Christ take on the seed of Abraham? Because it was necessary for Him to be a near kinsman to those He came to save (Matthew 1:21). For this reason St. Paul could say when writing to the Israelites at Ephesus: *"For we are members of his body, of his flesh, and of his bones"* *(Ephesians 5:30)*. Jesus Christ was a kinsman, an Israelite of the seed of Abraham. In the incarnation He took on the very nature, the *genetic seed*, of the people He came to save.

If salvation is for all races, the Law of Kinsman Redeemer must be waived, for God is forced to break His own law. Thus the Word of God would fail, and the honor and integrity of God's character would be at stake. If salvation were for all races, one could conclude that every race is genetically linked to Abraham. The church world has tried to circumvent the Law of Kinsman Redeemer by claiming that all who become believers in Christ are *spiritual Israel.* Most theologians are sufficiently versed in Scripture to know that Jesus Christ was the Redeemer promised to literal, physical Israel in the Old Testament. Moreover, they know that the New Testament establishes Jesus Christ as the Savior who came to redeem Israel (See Matthew 15:24, Luke 24:21, Acts 5:31, Acts 13:23, Romans 9;4-5, and Romans 15:8). Knowing that Scripture has clearly established a *genetic kinship* between Jesus Christ and physical Israel, the Church world has scrambled to invent a spiritual Israel to replace physical Israel. Because the Church world is unable or unwilling to identify physical Israel, they have not understood that the Gentiles of the New Testament are Israel in dispersion. Instead, they seek a better way to describe all those denominational, rank and file Christians: as spiritual Israelites.

The Law of Kinsman Redeemer does not allow a theology that embraces salvation for all races. People who push universalism in salvation must set aside the Law of Kinsman Redemption. Is there salvation for all races? Only Adamic creation was sold into the bond slavery of sin. Jesus Christ came to redeem or buy back those who were bondslaves to sin and death. Jesus Christ took on the seed of Abraham--no other seed! (Hebrews 2:16 and Matthew 1:21).

THE ATONEMENT WAS LIMITED AND DEFINITE

A major point for those who believe that salvation is for all races is that the atonement was for anyone who claims faith in Jesus Christ. Vast numbers of Christians view the atonement as unlimited and indefinite. In application, they perceive that the atonement reaches as far as necessary to include any one from any race who by faith in Jesus Christ is baptized. In contrast, the Bible teaches that the atonement was definite, particular, only for the people chosen in the election of God the Father. God designed and accomplished salvation through the substitutionary death of Jesus Christ. That death could be no broader than God the Father's will, plan, and design in election.

Most theologians and their followers are either **Armenian** or **Calvinistic** in their approach to how the atonement makes possible the saving grace of Jesus Christ. Arminians believe that Jesus Christ died for men of every race, without exception. They leave salvation entirely to man's free will, while God remains passive. In other words, God cannot save anyone without his or her cooperation. In contrast, Calvinists believe that God the Father has an elect group made from certain people from every race. No racial distinction is made. For Calvinists, atonement is definite for those who are in the election of God. All who are elect will come to God the Father. God will lose none of His children, but will draw every member of the elect to Jesus Christ for atonement from sin and will send the irresistible power of the Holy Spirit to turn their hearts to a life of faith and obedience.

The Bible teaches that God does have an elect group. God the Father will draw every member of the elect to a living faith in Jesus Christ and His atonement; the irresistible power of the Holy Spirit will empower every member of this elect group to come to the saving knowledge of God and be sanctified. The Bible teaches that God purposed a particular redemption for those numbered in His election. Who are the elect? They are those people chosen by God the Father before the world began to be redeemed by Christ. These elect are numbered in the remnant chosen of God in every generation, beginning with Adam-Noah (pre-flood history) and continuing from Shem to Abraham, Isaac, and Jacob Israel (post flood history). God our Father will not lose one sheep, one elect person. The blood of Jesus Christ will be effectual for those who are elect. The Holy Spirit will irresistibly draw every member of this elect to Jesus Christ for atonement, for no member of the elect can resist the Holy Spirit. What God the Father purposed in election will be made possible by the definite atonement of Jesus Christ.

What is definite atonement? It is limited atonement. The power of the atonement was not limited, but the design is limited. Jesus Christ died for a particular people, a people set apart for salvation and guaranteed to be saved. God the Father satisfied the justice of His immutable law totally in that the sin debt was paid by the vicarious sacrifice of Jesus Christ as the substitutionary lamb without spot upon the cross. Someone might say, "But I don't like the word *definite*." Would they rather have an *indefinite* or *incomplete* atonement?

The Bible teaches that the atonement was full; it satis-fied the justice of God completely. Since through Adam all men had come under the sentence of death for transgressing the law, God's perfect law demanded that the wounded majesty of God's honor be appeased. Restitution had to be made. This restitution required that a perfect sacrifice, a first born male without sin, be offered in atonement for sin. The atonement of Jesus Christ accomplished and fully sat-isfied the justice of God's law. It was a particular redemp-tion for a particular people whom the Father chose to set apart and save for Himself. Obviously, the opposite of a full atonement is an empty atonement. The atonement reaches as far as the electing grace of God wanted it to reach. To say that all races share in salvation is to give unlimited and indefinite force to the atonement. It places God the Father in a position of having *no election* and thereby invalidates the Holy Scriptures.

The nature of the limited atonement may be better un-derstood by a review of the *principle of substitution*. The atonement of Jesus Christ was a vicarious sacrifice. He took someone's place upon the cross. To appease the wrath of God and satisfy the justice of God's divine anger, Jesus Christ became a substitutionary offering for sin. He stood in the stead of those whom He came to save. Jesus Christ stood as a substitute in Israel's stead. The principle of sub-stitution is established in Romans 5:19: *"For as by one man's disobedience many were made sinners, so by the obedience of one shall many be made righteous."* Just as we are lost in sin by one man's (Adam's) disobedience, many are made righteous by the obedience of one, Jesus Christ.

The death of Jesus Christ upon the cross was a substitu-tionary sacrifice for a particular people. If we were to say that Jesus Christ died for all men to render them saveable, yet some perished, where is the substitution? But if we say

Jesus Christ came and stood in the stead for His people and fulfilled their responsibility in establishing the righteousness of the law, and that He died their cursed death and rendered satisfaction to divine justice on their behalf, it means that He stood where we should have. We are made acceptable by the substitutionary sacrifice of Jesus Christ. The atonement was definite and complete. God our Father will not lose one member of His election; no man can pluck them out of His hand (John 10:28-29).

Thus we can conclude that God our Father has chosen unto Himself a special people marked for salvation. Jesus Christ has redeemed these people from the curse of death by taking that curse and meeting the demands of the law in His vicarious sacrifice. The Holy Spirit has sanctified the elect and brought them to faith in Jesus Christ and repentance from dead works. No member of the elect will be lost. All will come to the saving knowledge of salvation by faith in Jesus Christ. The atonement is limited to the election of God. If there is salvation for all races, there is no election, and the atonement of Jesus Christ is indefinite and incomplete.

THE NEW COVENANT MADE FOR ONLY THE ELECT

A theology that embraces salvation for all races must find a way to *re-invent* the covenant theology of the Bible. A quick review of the Bible establishes that Jehovah made His covenant with Israel only. There is no provision in Scripture for all races sharing the covenant which Jehovah made with His people. This covenant consisting of the Ten Commandments, statutes, and judgements is graphically given in Exodus chapters 19-24. Israel rendered a failed performance in keeping the terms of the covenant; for persistent violation of this covenant law, they were judged severely by God. At the time that the Kingdom of Judah was under indictment for violating the covenant, God used the prophet Jeremiah to deliver an important prophecy. Israel of the Northern Kingdom by this time (B.C. 606) had long been divorced by Jehovah, and the Assyrian armies had transported millions of these Israelites in the land of the Medes and the Persians. The Kingdom of Judah, now involved in serious moral apostasy, was in serious violation of the covenant. At this point Jeremiah delivered the following prophesy:

"Behold, the days come, saith the LORD, that I will make a new covenant with the house of Israel, and with the house of Judah: Not according to the covenant that I made with their fathers in the day that I took them by the hand to bring them out of the land of Egypt; which my covenant they brake, although I was an husband unto them, saith the LORD: But this shall be the covenant that I will make with the house of Israel; After those days, saith the LORD, I will put my law in their inward parts, and write it in their hearts; and will be their God, and they shall be my people..." (Jeremiah 31:31-33).

The houses of Israel and Judah were promised a new covenant. There is no provision for other races to share in this covenant. The New Testament Scripture is the written confirmation of the covenant which God promised Israel. The opening chapter of Matthew gives a brief, working genealogy of the people chosen by God. The Gospels, Pauline Epistles, and General Epistles of the New Testament record the terms and provisions of the New Covenant promised by Jehovah to His people.

In looking at the record of the New Covenant, the people elected by God do not change. One people, the Israel of

God, are the subjects of the covenant in both the Old and New Testaments. You may wish to review the prophesy of Jeremiah as retold in the New Testament book of Hebrews.

"For if that first covenant had been faultless, then should no place have been sought for the second. For finding fault with them, he saith, Behold, the days come, saith the LORD, when I will make a new covenant with the house of Israel and with the house of Judah: No according to the covenant that I made with their fathers in the day when I took them by the hand to lead them out of the land of Egypt; because they continued not in my covenant, and I regarded them not, saith the LORD. For this is the covenant that I will make with the house of Israel after those days, saith the LORD: I will put my laws into their mind, and write them in their hearts: and I will be to them a God, and they shall be to me a people:"

There is never a word about the covenant being renewed with a different people. The new covenant remains with the people chosen by God the Father in the Old Testament.

The covenant of law exposed the sin nature of those chosen in election and convicted them under penalty of God's law. Jesus Christ came to die in their stead. The covenant is a record of the transaction made between God and His people. Israel failed utterly in her efforts to perform the requirements of the covenant. God the Father did not find fault with the covenant, for it was pure and holy (Romans 7:12). The fault lie in the people (Hebrews 8:8). By the vicarious, sacrificial death of Jesus Christ upon the cross, a new and better way of performing the terms of the covenant was made possible. That new and better way was the transforming power of the Holy Spirit. Under the terms of the New Covenant, the Holy Spirit made possible for the elect what had been purposed by God the Father for His children.

"Whereof the Holy Ghost also is a witness to us: for after that he had said before, This is the covenant that I will make with them after those days, saith the LORD, I will put my laws into their hearts, and in their minds will I write them; And their sins and iniquities will I remember no more" (Hebrews 10:15-17).

In truth, the Holy Ghost revealed Himself and inspired the Israelites under the New Covenant to perform the terms and requirements of the New Covenant. As a new creation in Jesus Christ, their righteousness came from God. Their obedience was by the operation of faith in Jesus Christ and the working of the Holy Spirit in their hearts and minds.

This New Covenant does not embrace all races of the earth, going no farther than the electing grace of God our Father. The terms and conditions of the New Covenant are limited to a particular people whom God had in mind from before the foundation of the world. The people of the new covenant have been made holy and blameless by the grace and mercy of a sovereign God, Who, working all things according to the counsel of His own will, purposed to save a people by the blood of His dear Son Jesus Christ. **Salvation is limited to the people who are named in the new covenant.** *"Jesus Christ is the same yesterday, and today, and for ever"* (Hebrews 13:7).

THE LAST WILL AND TESTAMENT CANNOT BE ALTERED

The Bible is a legal document recording the last will and testament of the Testator. God the Father is the author of the last will and testament, which we call the Bible. Being a legal document, the Bible sets forth the terms and provisions of the Testator to those who are heirs of salvation. All heirs are carefully named in this document. It cannot be altered and changed by anyone, including the Testator

(Malachi 3:6, Psalm 33:11, Hebrews 13:8). God has a list of every heir who belongs to this testament. Man cannot change the terms, conditions, or heirs of this legal document.

This testament was sealed by the blood of Jesus Christ. All the terms and conditions of this testament will be made effectual by the power of the Holy Spirit which proceeds from the Father through Jesus Christ (John 15:26). The terms of this testament have been validated by means of the death of Jesus Christ and His shed blood. A quick review of Hebrews 9:15-17 will help to clarify the importance of the last will and testament which God made in election.

"And for this cause he is the mediator of the new testament, that by means of death, for the redemption of the transgressions that were under the first testament, they which are called might receive the promise of eternal inheritance. For where a testament is, there must also of necessity be the death of a testator. For a testament is of force after men are dead: otherwise it is of no strength at all while the testator liveth" (Hebrews 9:15-17).

There has been no change in the last will and testament of the Living God. The Holy Bible has never been abrogated or invalidated. The Testator remains faithful and unchanging. The heirs of the testament have been purchased in blood, and no man can pluck them out of the Father's hand. What God has created and made clear, let no man change. The last will and testament of Jesus Christ is for those who are the elect of God the Father. If salvation is for all races, that last will and testament must be abolished, and a new Bible must be written. Who is ready to write a new Bible? Could that be why so many new translations of the Bible are now coming forth? Is the Bible being rewritten to encompass a program of salvation for all races? Let God be true and every man a liar. God's Word is unchangeable and infallible. God has spoken; His Word is true. Salvation is for those whom the Father chose in election before the world began.

THE BRIDE OF CHRIST IS NOT MULTI-RACIAL

If all races share in salvation, the bride of Christ would be multi-racial. The wife who is making herself ready for the Marriage Supper of the Lamb is not a multi-racial woman (Revelation 19:7-9). Rather, this wife is the same *racial* woman whom **Jehovah** married at Mt. Sinai. She is the redeemed seed of Abraham, Isaac, and Jacob Israel. Throughout the Old Testament, the imagery of the husband and the wife is portrayed in the relationship between God and the House of Israel. Isaiah, speaking of this relationship between **Jehovah**(the husband) and Israel (the wife), declares: *"For thy Maker is thine husband; the LORD of hosts is his name; and thy Redeemer the Holy One of Israel;...For the LORD hath called thee as a woman forsaken and grieved in spirit, and a wife of youth..."* (Isaiah 54:5-6). While lamenting the spiritual apostasy of Israel, Jeremiah declares: *"Turn, O backsliding children, saith the LORD; for I am married unto you..."* (Jeremiah 3:14).

In Jeremiah 3:1, the example of the husband and the married wife is again used to picture the relationship between Yahweh and His people Israel. *"They say, If a man put away his wife, and she go from him, and become another man's, shall he return unto her again? shall not that land be greatly polluted? but thou hast played the harlot with many lovers; yet return again to me, saith the LORD"* (Jeremiah 3:1). The Prophet Hosea, speaking of **Jehovah's** relationship with divorced Israel, uses the imagery of the husband/wife relationship also:

"And she shall follow after her lovers, but she shall not overtake them; and she shall seek them, but shall not find them: then shall she say, I will go and return to my first husband; for then was it better with me than now" (Hosea 2:7).

The love that existed between *Jehovah* and His bride in the Old Testament is an everlasting love. Hosea 2:19 speaks of this love in the following language: *"And I will betroth thee unto me for ever; yea, I will betroth thee unto me in righteousness, and in judgment, and in lovingkindness, and in mercies."* Jeremiah confirms that the love between *Jehovah* and Israel, his wife, is everlasting. *"the LORD hath appeared of old unto me, saying, Yea, I have loved thee with an everlasting love; therefore with lovingkindness have I drawn thee."*

The promise and hope which Israel, the divorced woman, is given in the Old Testament is a pledge of marriage. Israel, the married wife, divorced and sent into dispersion, is to be reunited with her husband. Ezekiel 37:21-28 is a prophesy calling for the complete reunification, regathering, and restoration of both houses--**Israel and Judah.** In that day Ezekiel declares that *"...they shall be my people, and I will be their God."* Hosea, speaking of this great day when Israel will be reunified, regathered, and restored into a Kingdom, declares: *"Then shall the children of Judah and the children of Israel be gathered together, and appoint themselves one head, and they shall come up out of the land: for great shall be the day of Jezreel"* (Hosea 1:11). Ezekiel, Hosea, and other prophets refer to the great event of the Marriage Supper of the Lamb as spoken of in Revelation 19:7-8:

"Let us be glad and rejoice, and give honour to him: for the marriage of the Lamb is come, and his wife hath made herself ready. And to her was granted that she

should be arrayed in fine linen, clean and white: for the fine linen is the righteousness of saints." The wife in Revelation 19:7 is the same woman whom the prophets speak of in the Old Testament. Both houses of Israel, Judah and Israel, were to be reunited, regathered, and restored under the headship of King Jesus Christ at His second coming. This would fulfill the declaration of the angel Gabriel as recorded in Luke 1:32-33: *"He shall be great, and shall be called the Son of the Highest: and the Lord God shall give unto him the throne of his father David: And he shall reign over the house of Jacob for ever; and of his kingdom there shall be no end."*

The wife of Revelation 17:9 will be eligible to be remarried to her former husband. Romans 7:1 and I Corinthians 39 declare that the wife is bound by the law as long as her husband liveth. The death of the husband is fulfilled in the passion, death, and burial of Jesus Christ. The married wife is now free to remarry. Jesus Christ, the resurrected, incarnate God, is the same husband whom Israel married at Mt. Sinai.

The church of the New Testament is Israel, and Israel is the church. The church of the Old Testament was Israel, and Israel continues to be the church of the New Testament. Theologians who teach that the Church is the body and Israel is the bride have not reconciled themselves to what Scripture teaches. The bride and the church in the Old Testament are one and the same people. Exodus 19:5-6 confirms that Israel was both the church and the state under covenant law. The tabernacle in the wilderness was composed of Israelite people. Nothing has changed in the New Testament. The church is the body, and the bride and Israel are that same people.

Those who want the church to be the body, made up of many races, and Israel to be the bride, made up of genetic Israel, are ready to enter into miscegenation. They want to bring their Church, a **multi-racial people,** into a marriage with **genetic Israel,** the people they call the bride. This would be pure folly and a violation of God's holy law. Israel is the Church. The Church is Israel. Israel is the bride, and the bride is Israel. There will be no separation of Church and State in the undivided government of God. If there is salvation for all races, the Marriage Supper of the Lamb will be a rainbow coalition. It would be a perfect New World Order social gathering. Sorry! This is not what the Bible teaches. Such folly would be blasphemy before the God who wrote the Bible. Salvation is not for all races, but for those who God the Father chose in election before the foundation of the world. The God of Scripture does not engage in wife swapping. *Jehovah* will **remarry** the wife of His first and only love. That people will be both His body and His bride.

IN CONCLUSION

Some twelve presuppositions have now been set for to demonstrate why all races do not share in salvation. This list could go on and on. For those who seek to build a house of faith on the Word of God, this will be a secure foundation. For those whose hearts are not content to build on Scripture, no amount of evidence will change their mind. Please give careful consideration and thought to the **twelve presuppositions** that have been given in outline form. As you review each of these presuppositions, take your Bible and try to prove them wrong. Make these presuppositions your very own by diligently studying the Word of God.

1) **The God of the Bible declares Himself to be the God of Abraham, Isaac, Jacob, and the twelve tribes.** Implication: If Scripture declares the God of the Bible to be the God of one special and particular people, by what authority does He become the God of all races of man?

2) **The Bible is the Book of Adam's Race.** Implication: If the Bible declares itself to be the Book of the Generations or race of Adam, how can it suddenly become the family history of every race on earth?

3) **There is no racial unity in Adam.** Implication: If Adam is not the father of all the distinct races on earth, how can all of these races share in the sin which God charges only to Adamic creation?

4) **All races were not placed under law.** Implication: If only Adam kind creation was placed under law, how can **sin** (transgression of the law) be charged to the races that were never under the law?

5) **The Election of God the Father included only one people.** Implication: If the Bible identifies by name and family history only one people to be the elect of God the Father, how can all the races and peoples of the earth become the elect? And what happens to the election of God the Father if the whole world becomes the elect?

6) **The adoption belongs only to divorced Israel in the dispersion.** Implication: If the adoption pertains only to Israel, how can one say that the other races are brought into salvation by means of the adoption or grafting in?

7) **The Gentiles are literal Israel in dispersion.** Implication: If the Gentiles are literal Israel in dispersion, how can the other races be brought into salvation under the name *gentiles*?

8) **The Law of Kinsman Redeemer defines those for whom Christ died.** Implication: How could Jesus Christ, being of the genetic seed of Abraham (Hebrews 2:16), qualify to be a kinsman for all races of the earth? If only a near kinsman could redeem someone sold into bondage (Leviticus 25:49), how could Jesus Christ redeem those not having any kinship with Him?

9) **The Atonement was limited to a definite, particular people.** Implication: If the atonement of Jesus Christ were limited to those chosen in election by God the Father, how could the atonement become unlimited and indefinite in its application for all those not in the election of God?

10) **The New Covenant was made only with the elect of God the Father.** Implication: If the New Covenant were to be made with only those specified in Scripture (Jeremiah 31:31-33 & Hebrews 8), how can all the other races be Scripturally justified as belonging to the New Covenant?

11) **The last will and testament of the Testator cannot be altered.**

Implication: The Bible is a legal document of which God Himself is the author. It is written to His elect. How can races not named in the last will and testament become heirs to the provisions set forth by the Testator?

12) **The bride of Christ is not multi-racial.**

Implication: If the bride of Jesus Christ is the same woman chosen in the Old Covenant, how can the bride of the New Covenant become another woman? How can the wife of the covenant suddenly become multi-racial?

DO NOT BEND THE KNEE TO BAAL

Powerful forces are moving against the living Church of Jesus Christ. Satan, the world, and sin nature are waging an eternal war to destroy the Church of the living God. The spirit of the age is pushing for the total integration, amalgamation, and mixing of the races. Satan and his minions are seeking to build a multi-racial church and join hand and heart with the New World Order. Tremendous social pressure is building to turn the church into a multi-cultural, multi-racial gathering center for every race, every religion, and every form of perversion known on earth. The total force of the news media, television, cinema, public education, government, and most pulpits is ablaze with this multi-cultural, multi-racial mania. Ridicule, ostracism, and persecution await all who will not **live politically and religiously correct** and join in building this modern tower of Babel.

However, the Christian remnant must not bow the knee to Baal! In the days of Ahab and Jezebel, one of the most wicked generations in history, *Jehovah* saved a remnant of some seven thousand Israelites who had not bowed the knee to Baal. Let *Jehovah* be praised for the Christian remnant of this generation that will not bow the knee to Baal and sacrifice their children on the altar of Baal. Praise God for the thousands of families who have purposed to remove their children from the multi-racial public schools and educate them in the moral and racial purity of their own homes. Thank and praise God for the many independent Christian Churches which have withdrawn from the Baal churches of this generation and purposed to remain morally and racially pure. May Jesus Christ be praised for the many thousands in Israel who look at the multi-racial, multi-cultural circus unfolding in America and upon bended knees repent of such baneful sin, purposing with God's unfailing help to have no part in it. *Pray that God the Father, by the grace of Jesus Christ and the aid of the Holy Spirit, will enable you and your household to not bow the knee to the Baal altars of this generation.*

WILL EZRA AND NEHEMIAH BE ALLOWED IN THE CHURCH?

In the days of ancient Israel following the return from the Babylonian captivity, the children of Israel had allowed themselves to buy stock in a multi-cultural, multi-racial society. They had begun to live among, socialize with, and inter-marry with the heathen people about them. The spirit of the age, much like our own, had seized upon the people. The order of the day was a public policy of integration and amalgamation of the races. There was a blending of the culture, customs, and religions of the diverse people living in the land. The Israelite people were being engulfed in this multi-racial, multi-cultural world of confusion. Into this race mixing, gender blending, perverted culture stepped a prophet of the living God. What did Ezra say and do? And, will the **Church of Jesus Christ** allow Ezra to come and give the same word today?

"Now when these things were done, the princes came to me, saying, The people of Israel, and the priests, and the Levites, have not separated themselves from the people of the lands, doing according to their abominations, even of the Canaanites, the Hittites, the Perizzites, the Jebusites, the Ammonites, the Moabites, the Egyptians, and the Amorites. For they have taken of their daughters for themselves, and for their sons: so that the holy seed have mingled themselves with the people of those lands: yea, the hand of the princes and rulers hath been chief in this trespass" (Ezra 9:1-2).

In the aftermath of this revelation, Ezra, in great spiritual distress and mourning, entered a time of fervent prayer. Falling upon his knees and lifting his hands unto *Jehovah*, He gave a prayer of great confession of sin as recorded in Ezra 9:6-15. Following this confession, made with weeping and mourning for the sins of the people, there assembled a great congregation of Israelites who, under conviction, were weeping and repenting before their God. Their response to the sins of race mixing, gender blending, perversion, and God knows what else was one of great importance. Hear what the living Church of that generation was saying:

"...We have trespassed against our God, and have taken strange wives of the people of the land: yet now there is hope in Israel concerning this thing. Now therefore let us make a covenant with our God to put away all the wives, and such as are born of them, according to the counsel of my lord, and of those that tremble at the commandment of our God; and let it be done according to the law."

Is the Church of Jesus Christ ready to follow in the steps of the convicted sinners of Ezra 10? Note what Ezra the priest tells the people: *"And Ezra the priest stood up, and said unto them, Ye have transgressed, and have taken strange wives, to increase the trespass of Israel. Now therefore make confession unto the LORD God of your fathers, and do his pleasure: and separate yourselves from the people of the land, and from the strange wives. Then all the congregation answered and said with a loud voice, As thou hast said, so must we do"* (Ezra 10:10-12).

If the Church of Jesus Christ continues to move toward a multi-racial, multi-cultural, gender blending, perverted church, will not God bring judgment upon the church? *"For the time is come that judgment must begin at the house of God: and if it first begin at us, what shall the end be of them that obey not the gospel of God? And if the righteous scarcely be saved, where shall the ungodly and the sinner appear?"*

Can the clergy of this generation continue to ignore the plain teaching of the Bible? Will the God of the Bible wink at the sin now proliferating in the Church? Will God turn His head and ignore the sins now taking place in the "Christian" community? The Word of God is clear: judgment will come, and it will begin at God's House.

Will we hearken to Scripture and bring revival, reformation, and spiritual renewal to the Church of the Living God? Will we continue to wallow in sin, teach salvation for all races, mix, amalgamate, and integrate until the wrath of God is poured out in great judgment upon His church? The day of decision is near. What will we do with so great a salvation? Will we give our spiritual birthright away for a mess of multi-racial, multi-cultural pottage? God forbid! With Joshua of old, shall we not say, *"...as for me and my house, we will serve the LORD"* *(Joshua 24:15)?*

Living Church, will we allow Ezra and Nehemiah into the church? Is it not a day to cleanse and purify the congregation? Is it not past time for mourning, weeping, and confession of sin? Is this not a day to do what the Bible records Israel did in the day of Nehemiah? *"Now it came to pass, when they had heard the law, that they separated from Israel all the mixed multitude"* *(Nehemiah 13:3). Can we do anything less?*

6

SETTING THE RECORD STRAIGHT

If you have made it this far, you are now ready for some plain talk. Having set forth basic Bible presuppositions on the matter of salvation history for the elect of God, it is time to set the record straight. What about the other races? If the salvation history as set forth in Scripture applies only to those in the election of God the Father, what about all those who are not in the election? The Bible declares that God works all things out according to the counsel of His own will (Ephesians 1:11). May we stand with St. Paul and declare, *"Who shall lay any thing to the charge of God's elect? It is God that justifieth"* (Romans 8:33). Who is man that he should question the sovereign nature of God's will? The salvation of the elect is the total work of a sovereign God who works in His children both to will and do his good pleasure (Philippians 2:13). Regarding the election of the sons of God, Scripture declares that they are those *"Which were born, not of blood, nor of the will of the flesh, nor of the will of man, but of God"* (John 1:13). God our Father who created all things by His own power, hath determined who will be saved. *"So then it is not of him that willeth, nor of him that runneth, but of God that sheweth mercy"* (Romans 9:16).

What is the place and purpose for the other races in the plan of God? Why are we unwilling to grant God the liberty of allowing all races to follow the unique purpose for which He created them? Why must we, Caucasians, mold every race into our own image? Why must we think that no race can exist happily unless they think and act as Caucasians? What gives Caucasian people, especially Christians, the justification for believing that all races must be poured into the religious mold of Christianity?

Consider this. Prior to the aftermath of the Protestant Reformation, the Caucasian Christian population of Europe showed zero interest in the conversion of other races to Christianity. There were no foreign missions assigned to the interior of Africa and Asia. The incessant proclivity to Christianize the non-white third world has been an obsession of the Christian West only a short time in the long span of history. The early 1600's marked the beginning of foreign missions to the non-white world by Christian Europe. The propaganda blitz that has followed the growth and development of rapid communication and transportation has greatly accelerated foreign mission activity in the Christian West. Most people cannot divorce themselves from the presuppositions that they were programmed to believe by the public schools, television, the pulpits, and news media. People today do not think like the Caucasian people once thought. Unfortunately, most view this generation as enlightened, broad-minded. We suffer from severe brainwashing. St. Paul describes our generation in II Timothy 3:7: *"Ever learning, and never able to come to the knowledge of the truth."* The more and better educated we become, the less we are able to discern truth. Why? Because **knowledge apart from the context of God and Scripture is foolishness (I Corinthians 3:19).**

We really do live in a world that is turned upside down. Truth has become the lie, while the lie has become the truth. White is black, and black is white. Truth has been cast into the streets, and the lie has been elevated into a position of honor. People who believe as Scripture teaches are considered mentally imbalanced, ignorant, unenlightened. People who hold to the Christian truth and traditions of their ancestors are marked as bigots by the liberal minds of this generation. Isaiah 5:20 makes this declaration: ***"Woe unto them that call evil good, and good evil; that put darkness for light, and light for darkness; that put bitter for sweet, and sweet for bitter!"*** Beware of thinking as the world thinks. One with God is always a majority. Do not follow a multitude to do evil (Exodus 23:2). The position taken by the media, most educators, and Hollywood will be wrong! Will you stand with the right?

Why do people become so sensitive about the salvation of other races? Why should Caucasians become alarmed about the salvation status of other races when the facts show that most of the Caucasian world is unconverted? One would tend to believe that people would first be concerned about "saving" their own kind! Instead, our tendency is to immediately question the spiritual status of the other races. Actually, every race has its own particular position to fill in God's plan. It is not for man to reinvent God's unique and perfect design for the races. Why not allow the non-Caucasian races to be what God ordained them? Why must we think that it is our duty to mold them into the spiritual mind set of the Caucasian race? In truth, the non-white races will always, after time, return to their manner of knowing and worshipping God. They were not created to know and worship God in the same manner as Caucasians. Can we not allow the master potter the power to form the clay as He so chooses (Isaiah 45:9-12)?

So, why do people become so disturbed when they find that the Bible is not the family history of the non-white races? After all, the Bible is not the family history of angels either. Angels are mentioned in the Bible, but they surely are not the focus of Scripture. There are many people, cultures, and nations included in the Bible, but the Bible is not the family history of all of them. Rather, it is the family history of those chosen in the election of God the Father. God has a place, a plan, and a design for every race. However, it is not for us to define that plan. Let God do it.

The world to come will be perfect and display all the diversity and contrast of the original creation. In its original design, every race will be represented in the restored Kingdom of God. Every species and kind within the original creation will be in the new heaven and new earth. There will be no hybrids, no violation of the basic law of kind after his kind. The Creator God will apportion every race its proper place on this earth. You may be certain that segregation of the races will be present in the perfect world to come. There will be no integration, amalgamation, and fusion of the races. A sovereign God will preserve His mark of ownership for every race.

To those who are really concerned about the place of other races in God's plan, both now and in the ages to come, please consider a few salient points. The non-white races were created before Adam, lived on the earth prior to the creation of Adam kind, and were created to live in a manner totally different from Adam. Everything that God created was very good (Genesis 1:31), including every distinct and separate race. **There is no justification whatever for racial hatred**. We are to respect and honor all of the creation that God has made. Representatives of all the animals, fowl, fish, and all other life forms (including all original races) will be present in the world to come. It is not possible to say which individual species of any of these life forms will be in the Kingdom, but that they will be there you may be sure--not as the elect to live forever with Christ, but as representatives of God's original design.

The time has come to set our theology in order in terms of salvation history. Caucasian Christians must rest content in converting their own kind. Foreign mission programs that involve the non-white, third world must come to an immediate end. The Christian West must set its theological house in order. The non-Adamic races did not share in the guilt of "original (birth) sin" and thus do not stand under the sentence of sin and judgment. Since they did not fall ethically with Adam, they need no redemption. Since they were not under law, they will not participate in judgment. The non-white races do not need salvation because they have nothing to be saved from. They are not under law and thereby are not under sin. Let us be content to allow the non-white races to know and worship God the Creator in their own form and manner. Let us not be foolish and believe that we must somehow force them to be made our spiritual equals.

All Christians must respect and honor the races that God created, however. There is no room for dishonoring them or showing contempt for that which God has created. As God's elect, we should remain humble and grateful. It is best for all races to pursue their own distinctive cultural patterns and God-given innate capacities. That every race would seek to live and dwell among their own kind is best for all concerned. In a multi-racial society where all the races are packed together by government decree, the purpose and plan of God is being purposely negated. In such a situation it is necessary for Christian people to carefully plan the path that they will walk. Christian parents can remove their children from the public schools, most of which are becoming multi-racial. They can home school their children or place them in all white, privately funded schools. You must live in those geographical areas where your kind are in the decided majority. Remove yourselves from those areas dominated my the non-white majority. Socialize and mix among those of your own kind. Worship in segregated Bible studies and churches. Be patient, be Christian, and never out of harmony with Scripture in your relationship to other races.

Do not surrender your racial and spiritual birthright for a mess of humanistic pottage. Do not allow temporary accolades from the world system to remove you from obedience and love of your God. God is not color blind, so why should you be? God is not ashamed of the color white, so why should you be? The white Caucasian male is an endangered species! Please do not contribute any further to the decline and death of the white race. Do not fail to love your own kind! Birds of a feather flock together. Even black birds know that it is best to be with other blackbirds. White egrets do not fool around with birds of another feather, and neither should you. Exercise wisdom, be kind, hold fast to the truth, and do not compromise the Gospel of Jesus Christ. Remain in the struggle for the long haul! This is a perilous day, and we must occupy till He comes (Luke 19:13). If that be six months, six years, or six hundred years, occupy and take dominion of the earth.

It may be important for Caucasians numbered in the Christian remnant to consider gathering themselves into covenant settlements. These **Christian Covenant Settlements** would allow families to settle in an area in privately owned homes and farms. They would have the opportunity to come together in segregated worship and socialize among their own kind without the presence of the non-white races. Their children could be raised among their own kind. These people would need to be creative, innovative, and extremely resourceful in building up trades, industry, and home based businesses that would allow for economic self-sufficiency. This is really a battle for the racial and spiritual survival of our people. If the Jews can segregate among their own kind, if the Black Muslims can congregate among their own kind, what keeps the Caucasians from doing likewise? If the Asians, Mexicans, and other ethnic groups can become exclusive from the primary population of a given area, what is to keep white people from doing the same?

Indeed, these are perilous days! No cause on earth can be greater than the spiritual and racial preservation of those distinct and separate races that God created. No matter how much humanism, propaganda, and brainwashing are initiated, there remains a racial consciousness among the various ethnic groups. Given the opportunity, most members of the non-white races would prefer to remain what God created them to be. Non-white races are not fond of watching members of their race marry outside their race. They innately seek to remain unto their own kind. It is only through the subtle brainwashing and humanism of public education, the cinema, television, sports, religion, and the media that people of all races are crossing the color line.

There is nothing to be gained from seeking to impose your views about segregation on other people, however. Concentrate on getting your own house in order. Look and see how you can improve the Christian walk in your own life. How about your children's Christian walk? Do not get caught up in any kind of racial conflict. There is no glory in causing any kind of racial tension. Separate unto your own people; stay among your own kind as much as humanly possible. If for any reason you have been misled into any form of race mixing, read Ezra and Nehemiah and do precisely what Scripture calls for you to do. Dissolve interracial marriages and let the offspring of such unions go with the parent who comes from the non-white race. Seek to fulfill your financial obligations for these offspring until they become of age. But, **do not continue to live in sin!** Follow the counsel of Ezra and Nehemiah! God and Scripture will always be right. Your intellect, your will, your emotions will probably be wrong. That is why people get into interracial relationships in the first place.

Parents have a strong obligation to train and educate their children and youth. They must be taught the plain truth about God and His Word on racial segregation. You dare not hide the truth from your children. Do not allow your children to become insensitive to the subject of race by allowing them to participate in integrated churches, schools, playgrounds, and sporting events. If your children are allowed to worship in an integrated church, do not be surprised at what may happen to your child as he or she grows into a young adult. When children grow up with non-white races in an integrated public school, they become insensitive to the condition of race. Parents who allow such socialization of their children are ripe for future interracial dating and marriage. Christian parents, wake up and smell the roses! Pull your heads out of the sand. You were born white because someone believed and practiced racial segregation. Can you do any less for your children?

Finally, why is there a burning desire to know about the salvation of the other races? Seldom do we show the same compassion for people of our own race. Our concern is not with our Caucasian neighbor, but the non-white at work, or on the basketball court, or at this nice church somewhere. One of several reasons why our people are so caught up in the urgent concern for the salvation of other races stems from misunderstanding Scripture. Our people are being destroyed for lack of knowledge. *"My people are destroyed for lack of knowledge: because thou hast rejected knowledge, I will also reject thee, that thou shalt be no priest to me: seeing thou hast forgotten the law of thy God, I will also forget thy children"* (Hosea 4:6).

All Christian people need to spend more time reading their Bibles and reflecting upon what God said rather than allowing themselves to be constantly bombarded by the television, cinema, and the newspapers. For example, suppose that every Christian carefully observed Matthew 7:6: *"Give not that which is holy unto the dogs, neither cast ye your pearls before swine, lest they trample them under their feet, and turn again and rend you."* I fear that far too many Christians are casting the pearls of the kingdom before those who do not need to know the Gospel. Let us not forget that the apostle Peter stated that the dog will return to his own vomit and the sow that was washed to the wallow. *"But it is happened unto them according to the true proverb, The dog is turned to his own vomit again; and the sow that was washed to her wallowing in the mire"* (II Peter 2:22).

Perhaps we need to give more careful attention to what God says in the Bible; maybe we should extend a lot less pity to those who are not candidates to hear the Gospel of the Kingdom. In John 10:26-27 Jesus Christ declared: *"But ye believe not, because ye are not of my sheep, as I said unto you. My sheep hear my voice, and I know them, and they follow me:"* If the testimony of many people in our generation is correct, Jesus Christ would need to render an apology to those people whom He did not consider proper candidates for His Gospel. Jesus Christ made it clear that only His sheep could hear the truth. Those who were not in the election did not hear because they were not His sheep. They were not his sheep because they did not believe. **They did not believe because they were not His sheep.** Too many people are lending their hearts to try and save those who are not numbered in the sheepfold. If any apology toward these other races is necessary, let God do it. We are merely His pawns on the earth. Remember that God is sovereign! Let Him accomplish His work on this earth, and let us be Christ-like and bear the fruits of the Holy Spirit. At the same time, let us work to separate from Babylon.

7

CLOSING THE LOOPHOLES

The purpose of this chapter is to close some loopholes that people use in an effort to include all races in salvation. That which follows is intended only for those who desire absolute truth in this theological matter. There will always be those who will accept nothing less than a theology that includes every race in the election of God, even if it means reinventing or rewriting the Bible. May our brief excursion into the following controversial Scriptures enhance your understanding of the Word of God.

If you understood well the previous Biblical presuppositions, the following discussion will seem redundant. Serious students of the Bible know that there are some fundamental laws that govern the science of **hermeneutics.** The interpretation of the Bible involves far more than just opening the Bible at random, lifting a verse out of context, and building a pretext that is foreign and isolated to the remainder of the Bible. Every verse in the Bible must be read in the context of the chapter or the book out of which it comes. And, in a greater sense, every verse of Scripture must be read and interpreted in the context of the entire Bible. The Bible is a unified whole. God speaks a unified Word from Genesis to Revelation. Moreover, a proper understanding of hermeneutics forbids building doctrine on isolated Scriptures that are not clear. Doctrine must be built in the mouth of two or three clear, unified witnesses in Scripture. My appeal is that those who are going to teach the Word of God prepare themselves with a well-developed study of hermeneutics. Do not undertake to build doctrine without submitting to the basic rules of Bible interpretation.

IN SEARCH OF THE 13ᵗʰ GATE

Many honest and sincere Christians are highly motivated to include all races in salvation. In an effort to build a salvation hedge around all races, they search from Genesis to Revelation for a way to get them all inside the Church of the Living God. Such is the case of those who are in a never ending search for the **thirteenth gate** into the holy city of the New Jerusalem.

"And there came unto me one of the seven angels which had the seven vials full of the seven last plagues, and talked with me, saying, Come hither, I will shew thee the bride, the Lamb's wife. And he carried me away in the spirit to a great and high mountain, and shewed me that great city, the holy Jerusalem, descending out of heaven from God, Having the glory of God: and her light was like unto a stone most precious, even like a jasper stone, clear as crystal; And had a wall great and high, and had twelve gates, and at the gates twelve angels, and names written thereon, which are the names of the twelve tribes of the children of Israel:" (Revelation 21:9-12)

The reader will note that there are only twelve gates into the Holy City of the New Jerusalem. **There is no thirteenth gate into the Holy City.** Those who are looking for a thirteenth gate through which the non-Israelite world may enter will need to look beyond Scripture to find that gate.

The redeemed of Jesus Christ will encompass only those who are marked in the election of God the Father, redeemed in the blood of Jesus Christ, and quickened and sanctified by the power of the Holy Spirit. There is no other entrance, no other doorway into the Holy City.

The bride of Revelation 21:9 is identified as the redeemed children of the twelve tribes of Israel. No amount of Bible study will change those who are chosen of God. The bride is Israel, and Israel is the bride. The Church is Israel, and Israel is the Church. The bride and the body are one people. The bride of Christ in the New Covenant remains the same woman that the Eternal married at Mt. Sinai. Israel was the wife in the Old Testament, and Israel is the bride that will meet Christ at the Marriage Supper of the Lamb in the coming Kingdom of God (Revelation 19:7-9 and 21:9-12). God is not going to replace His bride, chosen in election before the foundation of the world, for a multi-colored, rainbow wife of the New World Order. There is no thirteenth gate into the Holy City of the New Jerusalem; the people who make up that Holy City are those who have been redeemed in Jesus Christ from the twelve tribes of Israel and the covenant line from Adam to Noah and from Shem to Abraham, Isaac, and Jacob-Israel. Finally, examine Jeremiah 31:31-33 and note that the same people who were married to God in the Old Testament are heirs to the New Covenant. The bride and the Church are one people- *-if* you believe the Bible.

THE RITE OF CIRCUMCISION

The rite of circumcision is used by many to provide a Biblical context for the salvation of all races. The rationale for this position is built upon the supposition that baptism, like circumcision, becomes the seal of our standing with God the Father through faith in Jesus Christ. From this basic presupposition those advocating salvation of all races turn to Genesis 17 and point out that the rite of circumcision applied to all the seed of Abraham, including Ishmael, and all those in his house, even those not of his seed. From this rationale they simply say that any person, regardless of race, can become a member of the household of faith. By transferring the rite of circumcision as a seal of faith (Romans 4:11) under the Old Covenant to baptism under the New Covenant (Colossians 2:11-12), the road seems paved to include all races in salvation.

This logic, while used as a strong pillar for salvation for all races, will not stand the test of Biblical hermeneutics. Firstly, consider that the rite of circumcision of the foreskin marked only those who were the seed of Abraham, or those under his headship as in the case of those servants purchased with money. Circumcision of the flesh was not the equivalent of salvation. Consider that in the same chapter, the rite of circumcision is given to Abraham (Genesis 17); there is the pledge made by *Jehovah* of a **seed of promise** to Abraham and Sarah (Genesis 17:19). Moreover, there is the promise of an **everlasting covenant** to be made with this promised seed. (Genesis 17:19). Genesis 17:20-21 excludes Ishmael from this unconditional covenant made to Isaac, the seed of promise. *"But my covenant will I establish with Isaac, which Sarah shall bear unto thee at this set time in the next year"* (Genesis 17:21).

The circumcision of the flesh (foreskin) marked Abraham, his seed, and those of his household. This mark of circumcision was in all the seed of Abraham, that is all the seed of Ishmael, together with all those later born through Abraham's wife Keturah (Genesis 25:1-4). Indeed, multiplied millions of people on the earth today practice the rite of circumcision, and many of them would attach religious significance to this rite by virtue of their being descended from Abraham. It becomes necessary to look beyond the rite of circumcision of the foreskin in terms of determining salvation. This is evidenced in Genesis 17:19-21 wherein Abraham and Sarah are given the pledge of a **promised seed**; they are told that an everlasting (unconditional) covenant would be made with this seed. This covenant was exclusive to the promised seed (Isaac), and the blessings (salvation) did not accrue to those outside of this elect people.

The exclusive nature of this everlasting covenant is confirmed again in Genesis 21:9-12, where the bondwoman (Hagar) and her son (Ishmael), by the decree of God the Father in election, are ruled outside the covenant made with the promised seed: *"And Sarah saw the son of Hagar the Egyptian, which she had born unto Abraham, mocking. Wherefore she said unto Abraham, Cast out this bondwoman and her son: for the son of this bondwoman shall not be heir with my son, even with Isaac. And the thing was very grievous in Abraham's sight because of his son. And God said unto Abraham, Let it not be grievous in thy sight because of the lad, and because of thy bondwoman; in all that Sarah hath said unto thee, hearken unto her voice; for in Isaac shall thy seed by called."* Not only did this covenant exclude those not of the promised seed, but the emphatic declaration of God is that only in Isaac would the seed be called. This calling of the seed of Isaac, the promised seed, is a call to salvation. Indeed, the phrase *"In Isaac shall thy seed be called"* is repeated three times in Scripture: Genesis 21:12, Romans 9:7, and Hebrews 11:18.

St. Paul makes a strong case for the exclusive nature of the covenant made with Isaac, the seed of promise. In Romans 9:6-8 we read: *"Not as though the word of God hath taken none effect. For they are not all Israel, which are of Israel: Neither, because they are the seed of Abraham, are they all children: but, In Isaac shall thy seed be called. That is, They which are the children of the flesh, these are not the children of God: but the children of the promise are counted for the seed."* The implications of these words by St. Paul are tremendous. Only the children of the promise are counted for the seed and become subjects for salvation grace by faith in Jesus Christ. God's Word has not fallen to the ground. Those counted in the election of God the Father, the seed of promise, the children of Isaac, will be not be lost. The children of the flesh could be all of those who bear the mark of circumcision in the flesh, but still are not counted as the seed of promise. Paul continues to clearly define the seed of promise by further elaboration in Romans 9:9-11. The intent of the apostle was to show that *"...the purpose of God according to election might stand, not of works, but of him that calleth;).* The promise of salvation was made to a promised seed. That seed of promise did not include anyone outside the election of God.

Further investigation into Scripture reveals that the everlasting covenant made with the promised seed (Genesis 17:19, Romans 9:7-11) required more than a mark of circumcision in the flesh. The promise seed marked for salvation required a circumcision of the heart. The law and the prophets call the promised seed to a circumcision of the heart. *"Circumcise therefore the foreskin of your heart, and be no more stiffnecked"* *(Deuteronomy 10:12).* This circumcision of the heart is again confirmed in Deuteronomy 30:6 wherein *Jehovah*, speaking to Israel, the promised seed, declares: *"And the LORD thy God will circumcise thine heart, and the heart of thy seed, to love the LORD thy God with all thine heart, and with all thy soul, that thou mayest live."*

The prophets call the seed of Isaac, the Israel of God, living in the Kingdom of Judah, to a circumcision of the heart: *"Circumcise yourselves to the LORD, and take away the foreskins of your heart, ye men of Judah and inhabitants of Jerusalem:..." (Jeremiah 4:4).* Ezekiel calls Israel to a circumcision of the heart: *"...Repent, and turn yourselves from all your transgressions; so iniquity shall not be your ruin. Cast away from you all your transgressions, whereby ye have transgressed; and make you a new heart and a new spirit: for why will ye die, O house of Israel?" (Ezekiel 18:30-31).*

Jeremiah 9:25-26 contains a profound statement regarding circumcision of the heart. In these verses a contrast between circumcision of the flesh and the heart is made clear. *"Behold, the days come, saith the LORD, that I will punish all them which are circumcised with the uncircumcised; Egypt, and Judah, and Edom, and the children of Ammon, and Moab, and all that are in the utmost corners, that dwell in the wilderness: for all these nations are uncircumcised, and all the house of Israel are uncircumcised in the heart."* The implications of God's Word is clear. All of the other nations were uncircumcised in the flesh, but Israel remained **uncircumcised in the heart.** This circumcision of the heart finds its correlation in the act of Christian baptism which requires a new nature, a new heart, born from above by the transforming power of the Holy Spirit.

The connection between Christian baptism and circumcision is not that of the flesh, but of the condition of the heart. Paul speaks of this circumcision made without hands in Colossians 2:11-12: *"In whom also ye are circumcised with the circumcision made without hands, in putting off the body of the sins of the flesh by the circumcision of Christ: Buried with him in baptism, wherein also ye are risen with him through the faith of the operation of God, who hath raised him from the dead."* Christian baptism, then, is correlated to the circumcision of the heart rather than the flesh. Baptism, a condition for salvation, is for the seed of promise. Christian baptism is not necessary for those outside the election of God. In Isaac was the seed to be called, and those are the people which must have a circumcised heart.

The genetic link to those marked for election is clearly revealed in Romans 2:28-29: *"For he is not a Jew, (genetic Israelite), which is one outwardly; neither is that circumcision, which is outward in the flesh: But he is a Jew, which is one inwardly; and circumcision is that of the heart, in the spirit, and not in the letter; whose praise is not of men, but of God."* Those marked for salvation are not identified by a mark in the flesh. Millions may be marked with the circumcision of the flesh at any point in history. A genuine Israelite, a certified seed of promise, will be a person who is circumcised in the heart. Those who are in the election of God the Father must be circumcised in heart. They must have a new nature implanted in them by the power of the Holy Ghost. Only when this new nature is placed within them by the transforming power of God through the office and person of the Holy Spirit will they be circumcised in heart.

That circumcision of the heart is the true measurement by which the heirs of salvation are marked is found in Jeremiah 31:31-33. Here the prophet clearly expresses that a new covenant will be made with the House of Israel and the House of Judah (children of the promised seed), and the nature of this new covenant is that the heirs of salvation will have a circumcised heart. Again, the saving grace of Jesus Christ proceeds not from the mere fact of being marked by the outward form of circumcision, but by the transforming power of the circumcised heart. *"Behold, the days come, saith the Lᴏʀᴅ, that I will make a new covenant with the*

house of Israel, and with the house of Judah: Not ac-
cording to the covenant that I made with their fathers in
the day that I took them by the hand to bring them out
of the land of Egypt; which my covenant they brake,
although I was an husband unto them, saith the LORD:
But this shall be the covenant that I will make with the
house of Israel; After those days, saith the LORD, *I will*
put my law in their inward parts, and write it in their
hearts; and will be their God, and they shall be my
people" (Jeremiah 31:31-33).

The new covenant wherein *Jehovah* would write His law
was to be made with the House of Israel and Judah. It was
an exclusive covenant. The law was to be written in the
inward parts and in the heart. Both the soul (will, intellect,
and emotions) and the spirit were to be changed by the
transforming power of the Lord Jesus Christ. The earnest
down payment of this transforming power is documented in
Hebrews 10:15-16: *"Whereof the Holy Ghost also is a*
witness to us: for after that he had said before, This is
the covenant that I will make with them after those days,
saith the LORD, *I will put my laws into their hearts, and*
in their minds will I write them;" The new covenant was
made with those who were genetic, literal, real and visible
descendants of Isaac, the promised seed. Hebrews 8:8-13
names the people who were the subjects of the new covenant
promised in Jeremiah 31:31-33. They were the house of Israel
and the house of Judah.

In conclusion, there is no authority for using the outward mark of circumcision as the basis for extending salvation to all races. This theology will not fly. It falls to the
ground when tested in the true light of Scripture. The heirs
of salvation were to be marked in the flesh by outward
circumcision, as part of Abraham's family. But this had no
bearing on their salvation. The promised seed had to expe-

rience circumcision of the heart. A new spiritual heart transplant became a prerequisite for Christian baptism; hence, salvation by faith in Jesus Christ. The circumcision of the heart, and not the outward circumcision of the flesh, marks the true heirs of salvation in the purpose and plan of God.

WHO IS COMMANDED TO KEEP THE PASSOVER?

Many people, knowing that Passover is a central feast of the Bible and the Christian church, have endeavored to open salvation to all races through the door marked *Passover.* The Passover Lamb of the Old Covenant was a type of Jesus Christ, the Paschal Lamb of God. (I Corinthians 5:7-8, John 1:29, I Peter 1:18-19). *Jehovah* commanded the children of Israel to keep the Passover in anticipation of the coming redemption of Jesus Christ, the true Lamb of God. There is a direct correlation between Passover and the saving blood of Jesus Christ. Seizing upon this truth, advocates of salvation for all races seek to build the Passover celebration into something that is shared by all races. The Scripture most often used is Exodus 12:48: *"And when a stranger shall sojourn with thee, and will keep the passover to the Lord, let all his males be circumcised, and then let him come near and keep it; and he shall be as one that is born in the land: for no uncircumcised person shall eat thereof."*

This passage of Scripture must be read in the context of Exodus 12, and in a larger sense the context of the Book of Exodus and the entire Bible. This passage cannot be treated as an island removed from the mainland of the total Word of God. The proceeding verse, Exodus 12:47, declares: *"All the congregation of Israel shall keep it."* This verse most emphatically declares who the Passover is for. Moreover, other verses in this same chapter and elsewhere in Scripture define the kind of stranger who can celebrate the Passover. *Stranger* in the Old Testament has many shades of meaning. In Exodus 12:48 it refers to an Israelite that is born outside the land under discussion. Exodus 12:19 helps to clarify the meaning of *stranger*. It is simply an Israelite born outside the geographical limits of where the children of Israel were then dwelling.

Leviticus 25:35 confirms that a *stranger* or a *sojourner* can be classified as a racial brother (an Israelite). It simply means an Israelite born outside the land. Numbers 16:40 confirms that an Israelite not of the tribe of Levi could be considered a *stranger* in terms of those who were to offer incense unto **Jehovah**. Those who espouse the doctrine of salvation for all races hold that the act of Christian baptism will be all that is required for any person of any race to be Christian and thereby celebrate the Passover. The Bible makes it clear that the ordinance of the Passover was instituted for the children of Israel. Israel was commanded to keep the Passover among their *generations* forever. *"And this day shall be unto you for a memorial; and ye shall keep it a feast to the LORD throughout your generations; ye shall keep it a feast by an ordinance for ever...And ye shall observe this thing for an ordinance to thee and to thy sons forever"* (Exodus 12:14, 24). The Passover celebration is exclusive to those who are the elect of God the Father. A prerequisite for participating in the spiritual joy of the Passover feast is that you are a genetic Israelite, born anew by the transforming power of the Holy Ghost.

WHO ARE THE STRANGERS IN THE TEMPLE?

Many people, the clergy at the head of the pack, seek any door through which they may build a multi-racial congregation. So secure are these people in their multi-cultural, multi-racial pluralism that they are fast becoming the rule rather than the exception. In 1900, whites and blacks worshipped their Creator God in segregated houses of worship. It was unthinkable for the whites or the blacks to integrate in public houses of worship. It was done because the moral consciousness of our nation forbid the amalgamation of races in the Sanctuary of the Living God. This trend continued through the first half of the 20th century. The first step toward integration began in the military services during the Second World War. In 1945, American society was mostly segregated. Blacks and whites did not eat together in restaurants. They did not worship together. They did not share public restrooms. They did not live together. Interracial dating or marriage were unthinkable. Whites and blacks did not share the same educational facilities. America was a segregated society throughout the early years of the 20th century.

The post World War II years brought about rapid change in American society. Step by step the American population took on a form of color blindness by virtue of legislative statute by the United States Congress, judicial decrees by way of the Federal Courts, pressure from the liberal pulpits of most major institutional churches, and a choir of television and radio news commentators. All of this was greatly accelerated by the endless work of the Hollywood film producers who made movies that encouraged the integration and amalgamation of the races. By the end of the 1950's, a series of legislative statutes and court decrees, enforced by **tens of thousands** of United States military personnel, forced public educational facilities to open their doors to fully integrated schools, colleges, and universities. Liberal churches had already begun to open their doors to a fully integrated society. The United States Armed Forces, during the second World War (1939-1945), had begun gradually to implement the integration of the military services. By the end of 1964 and the passage of the **Civil Rights Act** of that year, American society was fully integrated. While millions of the American people were ready for full integration, those still unwilling to yield were made willing by brute police power of the Federal Government.

America is now a full generation into an integrated society. All of the social, educational, and religious institutions in the United States are fully integrated. Federal, State, and County governments are fully open to an integrated work force. All major corporations in the United States are fully integrated. Affirmative Action and racial quotas have mandated full integration. Only pockets of white segregated enclaves have survived the march toward racial amalgamation. Exclusive white suburbs still survive in the outer rings of many American cities. Vast regions of the American West, especially in the extreme northern tier of midwestern states, are populated whites. Elsewhere American society is moving toward full amalgamation and fusion of the races.

The institutional churches in America, beginning in the pre-Civil War days (1860-1865), had been working toward full integration of the races. The aftermath of the great Civil War has witnessed a powerful transformation of American society. The Bible has been pushed to the limits to make way for a fusion of the races into one racial family within the walls of the Living Church. The clergy has sorted and sifted through every verse and chapter, Genesis to Revelation, to find a door through which they can integrate the church. One such passage is that found in I Kings 8:41-43. This same series of verses is found in II Chronicles 6:32-33.

"Moreover concerning a stranger, that is not of thy people Israel, but cometh out of a far country for thy name's sake; (for they shall hear of thy great name, and

of thy strong hand, and of thy stretched out arm;) when he shall come and pray toward this house; Hear thou in heaven thy dwelling place, and do according to all that the stranger calleth to thee for: that all people of the earth may know thy name, to fear thee, as do thy people Israel; and that thy may know that this house, which I have builded, is called by thy name" (I Kings 8:41-43).

The stranger in this passage has been assumed to be a person of any color from any race who might want to enter the temple that Solomon dedicated to *Jehovah*, the God of Israel. The *stranger* in I Kings 8:41 and II Chronicles 6:32 must be interpreted in the context of all Scripture. It is unreasonable and Biblically incorrect to make broad assumptions about this verse by removing it from the context of the Bible. Firstly, the reader is reminded of a basic presupposition which the Bible declares of itself in Genesis 5:1-3. **The Bible is the book of the generations of Adam.** It is not the record of other races. Secondly, the reader is reminded that only Adam kind were placed under law and were responsible for original sin. None of the other races carried any liability for sin because they were not under the curse and penalty of the law. Thirdly, to demonstrate that Adam kind were under the law of sin and death and incapable of responding to God's call to righteousness apart from the election of God the Father, the redemption of Jesus Christ, and the power of the Holy Spirit, the Gospel was preached to every member of Adam kind.

Scripture teaches that there will be a resurrection of both the just and the unjust (Luke 14:14; John 5:28,29, I Corinthians 15:21-22). Every member of Adam's race must stand at the resurrection to be judged for the deeds of this life (II Corinthians 5:10, Romans 14:11-12). At the day of judgment, no member of Adam's race will be able to claim that they did not hear the saving Gospel of the Lord Jesus

Christ. *"For the grace of God that bringeth salvation hath appeared to all men"* *(Titus 2:11)*. The Bible clearly teaches that *"The Lord is not slack concerning his promise, as some men count slackness; but is longsuffering to us-ward, not willing that any should perish, but that all should come to repentance"* *(II Peter 3:9)*. *"Therefore, as by the offence of one judgment came upon all men to condemnation; even so by the righteousness of one the free gift came upon all men unto justification of life"* *(Romans 5:18)*. Scripture emphatically teaches that God gives all members of Adam kind the opportunity to be justified from original (birth) sin and their own actual sin by the saving grace of Jesus Christ. The God of Scripture is a God *"Who will have all men to be saved, and to come unto the knowledge of the truth"* *(I Timothy 2:4)*.

The elect of God the Father are called out of Adam kind. Every Israelite is an Adamite, but not every Adamite is an Israelite. The *strangers* that Solomon declared would come to pray in the temple who were not of the seed of Israel (I Kings 8:41-43) were those souls from Adam kind who were not Israelites. They were still members of the Caucasian race. The Queen of Sheba (I Kings 10) was of the nobility of Adam kind. The great city of Nineveh where Jonah was commissioned to preach belonged to Adam kind. They were descended from Asshur (Genesis 10:11, 22). All of these Adamites, (the people of Nineveh, the Queen of Sheba), as in Luke 11:30-32, will participate in the resurrection of the dead. All members of Adam's race will have no excuse on the day of judgment. They will all have heard.

The Gospel call will go out to all members of Adam kind. No member of Adam's race will be able to say on the day of resurrection and judgment that they did not hear. All will hear. Many will be called, but few will be chosen. Those chosen for salvation will be those who were purposed to be saved in Jesus Christ before the world began (Ephesians 1:4-5). The *strangers* who were to come into Solomon's temple were Adamites. They were not from the other non-Adamic, non-Caucasian races of the earth. In the light of this truth, one can see that the strangers of Ezekiel 44:7-9 are indeed all Caucasians from the race of Adam. All must hear the truth! Many Caucasians will hear the Gospel and receive it with joy. These non-Israelite strangers will give every appearance of hearing the Word and coming to the knowledge of the truth.

The Parable of the Sower (Matthew 13, Mark 4, Luke 8) confirms that only those who have ears to hear, continue in the Word, and bring forth fruit unto salvation will be saved. The Gospel is preached to the end that Israel, the elect of God the Father, can be called out of Adam kind. In the course of this preaching, **many strangers from Adam kind, not of the seed of Israel, will respond to the call, but their faith will not endure.** Not being the elect of God, they will fall by the way side, upon stony ground, or among thorns as in the Parable of the Sower.

The strangers who were prophesied to come into the temple that Solomon dedicated were not from the non-Caucasians of the earth. God's House is not a place of confusion. The sanctuary of the living God cannot be brought to shame and reproach. God and His Word must have a place of honor there. God has purposed for every race to worship Him according to the innate and unique capacities with which He created them. God did not purpose for all races to worship in one multi-racial congregation. This would bring shame and demise to every race God created. What God has created, let not the Church destroy. The strangers who come into God's house will not be of another race. They will all come from the Caucasian race. The Gospel of Jesus Christ will call Israel out of Adam. The others will fall into reprobation.

THE GENTILES OF ISAIAH 49

Those looking for a possible justification for the salvation of all races have endeavored to use Isaiah 49:6. They try to make the Gentiles in Isaiah 49:6 a people from every race and then join them with the Israelites to build a multi-racial church. Isaiah 49:5-6 reads: *"And now, saith the LORD that formed me from the womb to be his servant, to bring Jacob again to Him, Though Israel be not gathered, yet shall I be glorious in the eyes of the LORD, and my God shall be my strength. And he said, It is a light thing that thou shouldest be my servant to raise up the tribes of Jacob, and to restore the preserved of Israel: I will also give thee for a light to the Gentiles, that thou mayest be my salvation unto the end of the earth."* Isaiah 49 speaks of the office of Jesus Christ, the Messiah of Israel, and of the great salvation that He will bring to both Israel and the Gentiles.

The identification of the Gentiles is vital to understanding this passage of Scripture. If your presupposition is built from the idea that the Gentiles are non-Israelites, people of every race, you are on your way to a fusion of the races and a change of God's original design. If you followed our previous discussion about Gentiles in building proper Biblical presuppositions, you will have quite another foundation upon which to build. As previously outlined, the use of the word *Gentiles* in both Old and New Testaments has to be carefully sorted out. The Gentiles of Isaiah 49:6 are that branch of the House of Israel who were divorced from *Jehovah*, sent into dispersion, and cut off from the covenants of promise (Ephesians 2:12). Recall that Abraham was to become the father of many nations (Genesis 17:4-5). The word *nations* in Genesis 17:4-5 is translated into English from the Hebrew root word *Goy* and can mean Gentile, heathen, nation, or people. Abraham was to be the father of many gentiles or nations.

Millions of Israelites from the House of Israel were sent into dispersion and exiled among the nations under the power of the Assyrian Kings beginning B.C. 771 and ending B.C. 721. In confirmation of Hosea 1:10, this branch of the House of Israel was to be declared as a non-people (Gentiles) and were to lose their heritage as the children of God. They were to exist many days (years, centuries) without a king, without a prince, and without a sacrifice, image, ephod, and teraphim (Hosea 3:4). These Israelites, becoming a non-people, appeared under the name *Gentiles* in the New Testament era of Christianity. They were a Greek speaking people who quickly received the good news of the Gospel of Jesus Christ and became converts to Christianity.

Isaiah began to deliver his prophetic word just about the time that the Assyrian kings were beginning to make serious inroads into the Kingdom of the House of Israel, about B.C. 760. By the time that the prophetic word of Isaiah 49:6 was being delivered, the nation of Israel (Northern kingdom) had been carried away, as many as ten million captives, into the land of the Medes and Persians (II Kings 18:10-11). Isaiah, knowing that these millions of Israelites would be lost from the commonwealth of Israel, divorced from their God, and estranged from the covenants of promise, made the prediction that they would receive the light of Jesus Christ in all the nations of their dispersion. Hosea 1:10 confirms that the children of Israel, the very people who were carried into captivity and dispersed among the nations, would become the people who were not a people (Gentiles), and that one day, they would come to their spiritual inheritance and be called the sons of the living God.

It you take the position that the institutional church takes with Isaiah 49:6, this is what happens: God is incapable of keeping His covenant and promise to His people. Following His divorce of the kingdom of Israel (Jeremiah 3:8, Isaiah 50:1), God sought a replacement for the main body (ten tribes) of the House of Israel. These replacement people became the millions who would be recruited from all the other races of the earth. Under this plan, anyone from another race by a mere confession of faith in Jesus Christ could become a spiritual Israelite. Hence, the election of God the Father was a failed plan, and God was forced to reorganize His plans for genetic Israel around another people that He would call from all the other races. This forces God into a kind of **replacement theology.**

If you believe God and His Word, you will know that the people who were cast off, sent into dispersion, and left as exiles among the nations were not forsaken. God did not seek to replace them. A sovereign God could not lose His people. This is why St. Paul could say in Romans 11:1-2: *"I say then, Hath God cast away his people? God forbid. For I also am an Israelite, of the seed of Abraham, of the tribe of Benjamin. God hath not cast away his people which he foreknew..."* Because God had not cast away His people, James could write: *"James, a servant of God and of the Lord Jesus Christ, to the twelve tribes which are scattered abroad, greeting"* (James 1:1). The apostle Peter, writing to the Israelites of the diaspora (dispersion), could address his epistle to these people. He acknowledged that they were *"Elect according to the foreknowledge of God the Father, through sanctification of the Spirit, unto obedience and sprinkling of the blood of Jesus Christ: Grace unto you, and peace, be multiplied"* (I Peter 1:1-2).

The Gentiles of Isaiah 49:6 are a reference to the millions of genetic Israelites who were carried into the dispersion just a few years prior to this prophecy (Isaiah 46:9). The Holy Spirit, knowing that these Israelites would lose the knowledge of their God, His law, and their heritage, would simply refer to them as the nations or Gentiles as translated in the Authorized King James Bible. These Gentiles who were to come to the light of Jesus Christ, embrace the Gospel of salvation, and bring forth works meet for repentance were that portion of divorced Israel who had been dispersed among the nations. A sovereign God did not lose His people. There is no place for replacement theology! We must rightly divide the Word of God.

THE STRANGERS OF ISAIAH 56

Advocates of a multi-racial church love Isaiah 56. They view the strangers and eunuchs of Isaiah 56 as coming from every race in God's creation. Setting aside all the basic Bible presuppositions previously discussed in this book, these people are ready to forge new presuppositions and build their house of faith without regard to God's choice of a particular people called Israel. Israel can suddenly be enlarged to include all the world. By careful manipulation of Scripture, *Jehovah* is pictured as having changed His original design for Israel, and in discouragement and despair, He seeks to replace these impudent and unbelieving people with members of other races. For such people, a mere embracing of the covenant, a keeping of the Sabbath, and an expression of love for the God of Israel is all that is necessary for people of any race to become adopted, spiritual Israelites.

With such presuppositions, it is not difficult to see how the *stranger* and the *eunuch* of Isaiah can be viewed as being of any color in the rainbow. If, however, we hold fast to the Biblical presuppositions previously discussed in this book, Isaiah 56 becoming the grounds for building a multi-racial church fails miserably. Let us consider what Isaiah 56 is really about. Firstly, the *stranger* in Isaiah 56 is a foreigner, of another tribe, a heathen, one who is alien, or strange to Israel of the southern kingdom of Judah. This stranger is any Israelite from the Northern kingdom of Israel who was considered outcast by Israelites of the House or kingdom of Judah. Recall that a wall of partition had been erected between the House of Israel and the House of Judah. From the death of Solomon (B.C. 975) to the time that Isaiah was giving this prophecy (B.C. 712), some 260 years had passed. During this time there was a constant state of tension, hostility, and sometimes war between these opposing Houses of Israel.

Because the Southern kingdom of Judah viewed the House of Israel of the Northern kingdom as apostate and living in spiritual divorce from the temple, the sacrifices, the Levites, the feasts, the sabbath, and the God of Israel, they considered anyone from ten tribed Israel as heathen, uncircumcised, and therefore outcasts from the commonwealth of Israel. One might view the tension between these two Houses in much the same manner as the conflict between the North and the South in the great Civil War that nearly destroyed America in 1860-1865. You can imagine how the people of each side in this great conflict viewed each other. Such was this wall of partition between Judah and Israel in the days that Isaiah prophesied. Isaiah 9:21 and 11:13 speak of this growing enmity between Israel and Judah. Remember that Isaiah 56 is a prophesy of coming events. It is a forecast of a day wherein Israel of the northern Kingdom, cast off in divorce and sent into dispersion among the nations, will return to God. In such a condition (making their return to the covenant God of Israel), they would be considered strangers. They would be alien, foreigners, and heathen to the people of Judah. Being barren of spiritual life and estranged from their God (a dry tree), they would be likened unto *eunuchs*.

Isaiah 56:8 specifically addresses the fact that the out-casts of Israel (Israel of the Northern kingdom) will be gathered unto Him. At various intervals there were indi-viduals from the Northern kingdom who would return to the temple, the sacrifice, and the sabbath and become num-bered with the kingdom of Judah. When this occurred, these people were considered outcasts and strangers until they had fully completed all that was required of them. Isaiah 56:8 is referring to those Israelites, considered apostate and outcast, who would return to their God and the knowledge of His covenant and law, and that still others (future tense) would be gathered unto Him. This is a forecast of the great conversion that would come in the first century of the Christian era when vast numbers of these Greek speaking Israelites, outcasts to the southern Kingdom of Judah, would embrace Jesus Christ and return to the covenant of their God.

There is no room in Isaiah 56 for building a multi-racial church. The words *stranger* and *eunuch* can refer only to those Israelites lost in dispersion who would one day return to the knowledge of God, His covenant, and His law. Isaiah 56 must be read in the context of all the Book of Isaiah and in the larger context of the entire Bible. To believe that the stranger and the eunuch are people of other races is to completely forsake the great prophesies of the Bible that speak of the reunification, regathering, and restoration of the House of Israel in the earth. Without a clear vision and knowledge of both the House of Israel and the House of Judah, the student of Scripture is crippled when reading Isaiah 56 and related Scriptures in the Bible. You need not believe that the God of Israel had to admit failure with His people and go and find strangers from the non-Israelite world to complete His Kingdom. The God of the Bible has not lost His people. Only the clergy and their followers have lost the knowledge of who the strangers and eunuchs of Isaiah 56 are.

MATTHEW 28:19

Another Scripture often quoted as authority to take the Gospel to all races is Matthew 28:19, which states, *"Go ye therefore, and teach all nations, baptizing them in the name of the Father, and of the Son, and of the Holy Ghost."* If your presupposition for the word *nations* is that it includes people of every race and nation under heaven, you will feel comfortable in using this verse to build a multi-racial church. If you build your presuppositions from the Bible, it will not allow you to use this or any other verse to build a multi-racial church.

Just as with any other verse, Matthew 28:19 must be read in the context of the total Bible, Genesis to Revelation. A point of beginning would be to examine the multiplicity of seed that was promised to Abraham in Genesis 15:5. This seed then becomes the foundation for the many *nations* over which Abraham was to be the father in Genesis 17:5-6. In Jeremiah 31:1, *Jehovah* promised to be the God of all the families (nations) of Israel. The two families which *Jehovah* chose (Jeremiah 33:24) were Israel and Judah. Amos 3:1-2, in speaking of the children of Israel, declares: *"You only have I know of all the families of the earth:..."* (*Amos 3:2*). Jesus Christ declared in Matthew 15:24: *"...I am not sent but unto the lost sheep of the house of Israel."* Matthew 28:19 refers to the nations that would come from the loins of Father Abraham. The seed of promise was to come from Isaac (Genesis 21:12, Romans 9:7). The seed of Isaac was to number into the thousands of millions (Genesis 24:60) and be scattered over all the face of the earth.

That is why the Gospel of the Kingdom had to be preached in all the world for a witness unto all nations (Matthew 24:14).

Matthew 28:19 is a vital Scripture because it establishes the Great Commission. It cannot be separated from the mainland of the Bible. It cannot be divorced from Matthew 10:5-6: *"These twelve Jesus sent forth, and commanded them, saying, Go not into the way of the Gentiles, and into any city of the Samaritans enter ye not: But go rather to the lost sheep of the house of Israel."* The trail of Christianity will follow the tracks of Biblical Israel in the first centuries of the Christian era. The Great Commission was a call for both Judah and Israel, both Houses of Israel, to come to salvation by faith in Jesus Christ and repentance from dead works. Matthew 29:19 is not a call to go and preach to all races. It is the Gospel call to proclaim salvation to the two houses in Israel that are to be reunited, regathered, and restored by the saving grace of Jesus Christ.

MARK 16:15

Yet two other verses that those looking for a pretext to build a multi-racial Church have found consolation in are Mark 16:15 and Colossians 1:23. Mark 16:15 reads: *"And he said unto them, Go ye into all the world and preach the gospel to every creature."* Colossians 1:23 reads: *"If ye continue in the faith grounded and settled, and be not moved away from the hope of the gospel, which ye have heard, and which was preached to every creature which is under heaven; whereof I Paul am made a minister."* The word *creature* here is assumed to mean every person of any race under heaven. I have not heard of anyone claiming that the word *creature* might also include all the animals in the forest. Millions read Mark 16:15 and Colossians 1:23 believing that *creature* can be any person of any race with no regard to the election which God purposed in Christ before the foundation of the world (Ephesians 1:4-5, II Timothy 1:9).

The Greek root words *ktisis* and *ktisma*, translated *creature* in the Authorized King James Bible, give no authority for including all races in the salvation history of the Bible. The word *creature* is not without qualification and limitation. It does not include every creature God made, nor every race. Rather, it has to do with those who are the subjects of the Bible. Who are they? Genesis 1:26-27 names these people who are of the Adamic creation. Genesis 5:1-2 establishes that the Bible is the record or family history of these people. Deuteronomy 32:8-9 establishes that Adam kind, specifically Israel, are these people. To believe that the word *creature* can be lifted out of the context of God's Word is unreasonable and has no Biblical foundation.

The implication of Mark 16:15 and Colossians 1:23 is clear. The Gospel is to be preached to every creature after Adam's kind. Because Adam kind is dispersed throughout the world, the Gospel must be preached throughout the world. It is that simple. Isaiah 27:6 declares that the seed of Israel will fill the face of the world with fruit, people; therefore, the Gospel must be preached world wide to reach all the Israelites. *Creature* has reference to the original formation of Adam man, made in the image and likeness of God. To include every race in the context of the manner in which creature is used would be casting asunder all the pillars of Bible truth. God and Scripture cannot be used to justify a multi-racial church. Only Satan, the world, and sin nature will justify the integration of God's House and the interracial dating and marriage that follows such insanity.

ACTS 17:26

Another popular and well worn verse of Scripture used to justify the call to universal salvation is Acts 17:26, which reads as follows: *"And hath made of one blood all nations of men for to dwell on all the face of the earth, and hath determined the times before appointed, and the bounds of their habitation."* Not to sound redundant, this verse cannot be separated from the mainland of Scripture. To say that all races share one bloodline is absurd! Acts 17:26 is a paraphrase by St. Paul of Deuteronomy 32:8-9. The reader will do well to give careful attention to this Scripture.

"When the Most High divided to the nations their inheritance, when he separated the sons of Adam, he set the bounds of the people according to the number of the children of Israel. For the LORD's portion is his people; Jacob is the lot of his inheritance." This is the verse that is paraphrased in Acts 17:26. Notice that only Adam kind is under consideration. Israel is that special portion or inheritance that God chose in election to be the subjects of salvation history. All of the Adamic nations on earth descend from one bloodline: Adam's. To read anything else into Acts 17:26 is to remove this verse from the context of Scripture and turn the Word of God into a theological shambles. No person can open the Bible to any given verse and read it out of the context of the total Word of God. Every verse of Scripture must be viewed in the light of what Scripture teaches. Acts 17:26 simply says that out of one man-- Adam--God made all the nations of Adam kind. Our magnificent God determined the bounds of their habitation and established them in the time schedule of His divine calendar.

REVELATION 5:9

Revelation 5:9, 7:9, and 14:6 speak of one people, the elect of God. The author of the Revelation Letter had one people in mind when he described the events of Revelation 5:9, 7:9 and 14:6. He was speaking of the heirs of salvation, the subjects for whom Jesus Christ died. To try to fuse the races into a multi-racial church and gather a mixed multitude into the House of God is not possible. The Revelation Letter cannot be used to justify the spiritual marriage of all races into one Living Church. Jesus Christ did redeem His elect from the various Israelite nations which have descended from the Adam kind. These Israelite nations have spoken a great diversity of tongues (languages) in their historical development. Many diverse customs and qualities make up the Israelite family of nations. The key word used in Revelation 5:9, 7:9, and 14:6 is *kindred*. If you are able to define this word, you will not be able to turn these Scriptures into justification for building a multi-racial church.

The word *kindred* is #5443, *Foo-lay*, Race, or clan, kindred, or tribe. The very meaning and definition of the word *kindred* places limitations on the meaning of Revelation 5:9, 7:9, and 14:6. Notice the reading of Revelation 5:9: ***"And they sung a new song, saying, Thou art worthy to take the book, and to open the seals thereof: for thou wast slain, and hast redeemed us to God by thy blood out of every kindred, and tongue, and people, and nation."*** The word *kindred* clearly confirms that all those people with differing tongues (languages) are a kindred people, coming from the same racial stock. Careful examination of the religion of Christianity will reveal that this particular faith has always traveled with a people who speak different tongues, have their own unique culture and customs, and share a common bond of racial and spiritual affinity. I speak of the Anglo, Saxon, Celtic, Germanic, and *kindred* people who historically have been the builders of the Christian West. Christianity has traveled always and forever within the limitations of the Anglo, Saxon, Celtic, Germanic and kindred people, the standard bearers of the Christian faith.

The **Random House Dictionary of the English Language** defines the word *kindred* as 1. "a body of persons related to another; family, tribe, or race. 2. One's relatives collectively; kinfolk; kin. 3. Relationship by birth or descent, or sometimes by marriage; kinship. 4. Natural relationship, affinity. 5. Associated by origin, nature, qualities, etc. kindred languages."

The **Oxford Universal Dictionary,** Oxford at the Clarendon Press, 1933, defines *kindred* as follows: "**KINDRED. 1. The being of kin; relationship by blood (occas., but erron., by marriage); kinship....Of the same kin; related by birth or descent 1530...Belonging to, existing between, or done by, relatives...**"

The Revelation Letter cannot be used to justify a multi-racial church. Jesus Christ did not write a love letter to a multi-racial bride. Those redeemed in the blood of Jesus Christ and recorded in Revelation 5:9, 7:9, and 14:4 are all of the same blood. They are a kindred people sharing a blood relationship in Abraham, Isaac, Jacob, and the twelve tribes. There is no 13th gate into the Holy City for a **rainbow coalition.** The mixed multitude which now gathers in the House of the Living God does not have His blessing upon them. We are warned in I Peter 4:17-18 that judgment must begin at God's House. Judgement is already falling on the House of God; His wrath has only begun to be felt. May God, in His infinite mercy, grant repentance to His people so that the Sanctuary may be cleansed and spared the certain judgment that is to come.

JEHOVAH IS THE GOD OF ONE PEOPLE

People who wish for a multi-racial church would have you believe that *Jehovah*, the God of Israel, is somehow the God of all people of the earth. The Bible does not teach this to be true. Indeed, Micah 4:5, speaking of the restored Kingdom of God on earth, has this to say about how God will be worshipped. *"For all people will walk every one in the name of his god, and we will walk in the name of the LORD our God for ever and ever."* Micah makes it clear that all the various people who occupy the earth in the Kingdom will not know *Jehovah*, the God of Israel. *Jehovah* is the God of Abraham, Isaac, and Jacob Israel. This does not mean that all the other people on earth may not know God or worship him. Every people can know and worship God in some manner. However, **only Israel walks in covenant relationship with *Jehovah*.**

8

THE PRESENT CRISIS

The Changing Racial Face of America

"O Eternal, to us belongeth confusion of face, to our kings, to our princes, and to our fathers, because we have sinned against thee. Neither have we obeyed the voice of the LORD our God, to walk in his laws, which he set before us by his servants the prophets" (Daniel 9:8-9).

The Caucasian populace of America is being swallowed in a sea of color. A tidal wave of third world immigrants swarms the shores of the United States and the Dominion of Canada. They are coming from the far ends of the earth, arriving by land, sea, and air every day of the week. Millions in Asia, India, Africa, South and Central America, and Mexico have their eyes riveted on the paradise they believe America to be. They are determined to help themselves to the material abundance and economic affluence that they see via television and other forms of mass media. The arrival of millions of people from throughout the third world is changing the racial face of America. Asians and Mexicans have already over run the Southwestern United States. The browning of Texas, Colorado, New Mexico, Arizona, and California is well under way. The population of Mexico City, one of the largest cities on earth, is transplanting its millions to American cities. Europe, the British Isles, and Australia are faced with this same tidal wave of third world people.

Enthralled with the hope of a better life and infused with the idea that once they arrive on American soil, they can experience a materialistic utopia, the huddled masses from Asia, India, Africa, and South and Central America flock to American shores. They arrive by air, come by rusty boats, and walk across the American/Mexican border in broad daylight. Major American cities already express the racial countenance of the third world. San Diego and Los Angeles appear as full fledged Mexican cities, out of place in a former Caucasian land. San Francisco and Seattle appear as extensions of the Asian mainland. A Caucasian is fast becoming an endangered species in many of America's largest cities. The American "camp of the saints" is rapidly becoming the land of the mixed multitude.

Immigration of the third world into the United States is out of control. The United States Immigration Service stands helpless in the face of this tidal wave of color. We stand imperiled and incapable of knowing how to hold back this relentless population advance. Like a giant glacier moving everything in its path, this movement of people from the third world is changing the political, economic, social, religious, spiritual, and racial face of America. Caucasian children born in America at the end of the 20th century will witness the squalor, disease, deprivation, and horrendous suffering of a third world nation before they grow old. The racial confusion of face is apparent on every sidewalk and market place in American society. The color white is being lost amid the sea of black, brown, and yellow faces that fill the urban landscape. In time, the vast, white, rural areas of America will find themselves buried in the avalanche of

Asian, African, Indian, and Mexican blood currently popu-
lating American cities.

Confusion of face is not limited to America and the
Dominion of Canada. Europe, the British Isles, and
Scandinavia are all targeted by the huddled masses of
Jakarta, Karachi, Conakry, and the millions living in the
squalor and disease of sub-Saharan Africa. Africa, the Third
World's Third World, is in a state of environmental devas-
tation, social collapse, mass unemployment, and rapid population growth. One can almost envision a mass migration of
these millions over land, across the Straits of Gibraltar, and
on into the European fatherland. It is difficult to imagine
how Switzerland, with an annual average per capita income of about $35,000, can stay the flood of third world
people whose average income is less than $300. The march
on Europe has already begun, and the changing racial face
of almost every European city is painfully evident. In 1950,
The United States and Europe contained about 22 percent
of the world's population. That figure will drop to about
10% by 2025. The goal of liberal politicians and world plan-
ners is to create a borderless world. The wealthy elite will
build protective, armed walls around their riches and then
welcome the third world to share the wealth and property
of everyone else.

The ever growing presence of third world people has
placed the Caucasian population of America and Europe in
great peril. Firstly, the presence of this surging population
advance upon our shores is threatening the present and
future welfare of our country. Secondly, our own American
population is becoming insensitive-- even numb--to the threat
of the third world avalanche. Growing millions of Caucasians are unwilling to examine the danger now facing them;
ever greater numbers simply do not care. The Caucasian
race in America has lost the will to battle for the preserva-

tion of their kind. The American clergy, educators, politicians, and civic leaders have already surrendered any hope of preserving a Christian and Caucasian culture in the United States of America. These people have already cast their die! They want a total melting pot, the complete fusion of the races, and a society that makes a place for every god, religion, race, and ideology known on earth.

Long cherished standards of racial purity, ethnic pride, and Christian morality are being surrendered, if not squandered, in wholesale fashion by the clergy, fathers, politicians, educators, and media masters of contemporary America. Miscegenation, once considered a curse and punished by statutory law, is now a cherished pastime with the American people. Men of every color now openly court Caucasian girls. The children being born to interracially mixed couples number into the hundreds of thousands. The racial face of America is changing, and white is not the color emerging from this moral chaos. Minsters by the thousands foster and push for full, racial amalgamation of the American population. Long established standards of racial segregation gave way to integration in the 1950's and 1960's. Since the goal to integrate American society has been achieved, the push now is for the full racial amalgamation of the Caucasian population into the non-white racial river now overflowing its banks throughout America.

Now it does little good to blame the racial peril now facing America on the people arriving from the third world. The blame must be placed where it really belongs: on ministers, fathers, and civil leaders--in that order. Having removed the long standing Biblical principles that call for racial segregation and the practice of the law of kind after his kind, there are now no moral restraints to hold back the total amalgamation of the third world into the racial seedbed of the American nation. Caucasian Christians have broken covenant with God. They have forsaken basic Bible principles that once held the racial integrity of America in place. Having done so, they are incapable of holding back the national mania of the Caucasian drive to integrate, mix, amalgamate, and scramble the gene pool that has, by the unfailing help of God our Father and His Son Jesus Christ, built the Western Christian culture in America.

The Christian underpinning of America has long since been removed from our society. The Ten Commandments have been discarded from the pulpits, the classrooms, the courtrooms, and worst of all, the hearts and minds of the American people. The absolutes of God's moral laws, once cherished and revered, have now been trashed by a generation who does not know the God of Abraham, Isaac, and Jacob-Israel. Having divorced themselves from God and Scripture, the American public has reared new gods and fallen in love with humanism. The idols of the new morality can be observed everywhere in America. The great coliseums and sporting events draw millions to their altars. The demon of lust has captured and stolen the hearts of the American public. Nakedness and lust of every form are displayed on billboards throughout the nation, and television and movie screens portray an endless program of sex, violence, perversion, and immorality.

The American nation has been sowing the seeds of racial amalgamation for many generations. We are now beginning to reap what we have sown: the bitter harvest is appearing. Racial confusion covers our land. Tens of thousands of people can no longer be identified as one particular race. Instead they are a composite of many races. Utter confusion! They are the direct result of what happens when a basic law of Scripture, the **law of kind after his kind** (mentioned ten times in Genesis 1) is discarded by any people. It is not unusual for a face that demonstrates Asian,

Negroid, Mexican, and Caucasian features to appear in American society. The mongrel offspring of interracial marriages, once considered unacceptable in American society, now are openly welcomed. They represent the new standard of racial integrity. There are no rules that govern racial integrity in America. Anything is acceptable. Every form of racial amalgamation is now the "in thing." The Caucasian population has elected to pursue a course of racial suicide, and there appears to be nothing that can stop it.

Current racial policies and practices in American society are bringing about the demise of every race. God's mark of ownership in every race is disappearing in the sin of miscegenation. The integrity and unique qualities of every race are being lost in the mania of mixing, mating, and amalgamating. In the beginning God made man in His own image and after His own likeness (Genesis 1:26,27). Modern man is remaking man in the image of the new god of human reason. "If it feels good, do it!" is the new American psyche. We dare not commit racial suicide in the West. The Caucasian people, having abandoned God and Scripture, broken His covenant, and loved, served, and worshipped other gods, are the guilty parties in this national race to suicide. Anyone who opposes the complete integration and amalgamation of the races is targeted for ridicule and persecution and becomes charged with racism and bigotry.

Every person of color is given great liberty in American society to display their racial preferences and tout their prejudice in favor of their particular color and race. The Caucasians have no such privilege, however. They dare not express pride for their race. No Caucasian is allowed to defend his heritage and the ethnic gene pool that built and made all of western Christian civilization, including the United States of America. The total force of American society comes down on any Caucasian who dares stand for the integrity of the race into which he was born. Persons of every other color and race can flaunt racial prejudice to the high heaves and be applauded in doing so. Not so with Caucasians. They must hide in the dens and caves of society and never allow their feelings for their heritage and ethnic pride surface amid the rising tide of color. There is a place setting for every race in the democratization of American society, but not for Caucasians. White is not beautiful anymore. White is irrelevant! White can only be tolerated when it is willing to be merged in a rainbow of racial colors.

The American western Christian civilization is moving toward racial suicide. Our economic, political, social, and religious problems pale into insignificance beside the problem of racial suicide. Indeed our crumbling, faltering economic, political, and social fortunes are directly correlated to the changing racial face of America. The more confusion of racial face that we take on, the more compounding our political, economic, social, and moral problems escalate. The enemy is not only at the gates; the enemy stands in control of the future of our children. In the midst of this national peril, we continue in our mad rush to suicide without a thought for national repentance, turning to the God of our fathers, and restoring ourselves under His righteous law. The confusion of face now abounding in America is a silent witness that this nation has willed to die.

The mingling of the Caucasian people with the gods, temples, and genes of other races has long been a **sin** of our people. The Psalmist David declared this sin among the Israel people. Describing this iniquity David declared that Israel *"...mingled among the heathen, and learned their works. And they served their idols: which were a snare unto them. Yea, they sacrificed their sons and their daughters unto devils. And shed innocent blood, even the* *blood of their sons and of their daughters, whom they sacrificed unto the idols of Canaan:.."* *(Psalms 106:35-38)*. Indeed the Caucasian people, upon leaving Egypt at the time of the exodus, were followed by the mixed multitude. *"And a mixed multitude went up also with them; and flocks, and herds, even very much cattle"* *(Exodus 12:38)*.

In the unfolding generations this mingling, mixing, and amalgamating could inspire *Jehovah* to speak through His servant Jeremiah and declare: *"Yet I had planted thee a noble vine, wholly a right seed: how then art thou turned into the degenerate plant of a strange vine unto me? For though thou wash thee with nitre, and take thee much soap, yet thine iniquity is marked before me, saith the Lord God"* *(Jeremiah 2:21-22)*. The iniquity of race mixing is marked on the faces and the gene pool forever. Neither soap nor repentance can erase the curse and scourge of what happens to any race that sacrifices their sons and daughters on the altar of miscegenation.

Years later the Prophet Jeremiah could give this prophesy concerning the Caucasian people who were called Israel in the Old Testament. *"Behold, the days come, saith the Lord, that I will sow the house of Israel and the house of Judah with the seed of man, and with the seed of beast"* *(Jeremiah 31:27)*. First the Israelites **in sin** would mix with the Adamic nations about them. Later, they would fully surrender their racial and moral heritage by mixing with the beast. This prophesy is literally taking place in the public schools, college classrooms, sport coliseums, and churches in contemporary America. In the days of Ezra, remorse for sin was sufficiently strong for Ezra and his people to put away the shame of miscegenation by divorce and separation. *"Now therefore let us make a covenant with our God to put away all the wives, and such as are* *born to them,...and let it be done according to the law"* (*Ezra 10:3*).

Later, in a time when the consciences of our people were pricked with the shame of sin, they were ready to receive this message from the lips of Nehemiah: *"Now it came to pass, when they had heard the law, that they separated from Israel all the mixed multitude"* (*Nehemiah 13:3*). O that God would give us another Jeremiah, another Ezra or Nehemiah, and that our people, filled with shame and remorse for **sin,** would repent and restore themselves under God and His law! I fear that it may be too late for America to turn back. The God of Scripture may very well judge America and save only a righteous and racially pure remnant as He did in the days of Noah (Genesis 6:9).

WHAT MUST WE DO?

The hour is late and time is of the essence. Following are the steps that every Christian, Caucasian family must take in this time of national peril. Firstly, get inside the Ark. The Ark may be described as the Church of Jesus Christ where His blood becomes the only atonement for sin and His law becomes the only standard by which we live. Find yourselves a Church where Jesus Christ, His grace and law, and racial purity remain a cornerstone of the faith. Flee any church body and minister who compromise racial integrity for temporary expediency and popularity. Associate with a body of believers whose personal, family, and church vision encompasses a racially pure future for their children and grandchildren. Flee a church body whose ministers will not preach the truth of Ezra, Nehemiah, and other books in Scripture that forbid miscegenation.

Secondly, move forth with a vision for your personal family. Once you have removed yourselves from a racially mixed church, move forth in other areas of your family life.

Remove your children from the public schools, and home school your children or provide a setting for private tutoring. **Beware of so-called Christian schools.** Many Christian schools build their student body from the dregs that are expelled from the public schools. Remove your children from the baneful influences found in the world, especially rock music, the cinema and television screen, and all glorified heroes in the world of sports. Remove yourselves from the geographical center of race mixing. Locate in those areas where your kind of people still are the majority. Hold your standards high. Inform, educate, and instill in your children a love for God and their ethnic heritage. Work hard to educate and witness to your good Caucasian neighbors. Let the training of your racially pure *Christian* children become the highest priority of your work and vision in life. **Work hard to increase the physical size and spiritual strength of the Christian family.**

Finally, it is imperative to remember that we have lost our place in history through default. Sin has robbed us of the former grandeur and glory of America. The iniquities of our fathers and our own sin have placed us in great jeopardy with *Jehovah*. Our only remedy is repentance, confession of sin, and turning to Jesus Christ for atonement for sin and the righteousness of His law as the only standard by which we live. We must quietly, peaceably, work to build the Ark (the Christian Church); with all of our might and strength, we must build the **Christian family** in our generation. Let us resolve to let our children be the final proof of our Christian life and work on this earth. Work as if it all depended upon you, and pray as if it all depended upon God. Finally, remember what Jesus Christ declared in Luke 12:32: *"Fear not, little flock; for it is your Father's good pleasure to give you the kingdom."*

9

THE ORIGIN OF THE RACES

"When the Most High divided to the nations their inheritance, when he separated the sons of Adam, he set the bounds of the people according to the number of the children of Israel. For the LORD's portion is his people; Jacob is the lot of his inheritance" (Deut. 32:8-9). *"For the LORD hath chosen Jacob unto himself, and Israel for his peculiar treasure"* (Psalm 135:4). *"And what one nation in the earth is like thy people, even like Israel, whom God went to redeem for a people to himself, and to make him a name, and to do for you great things and terrible, for thy land, before thy people, which thou redeemst to thee from Egypt, from the nations and their gods? For thou hast confirmed to thyself thy people Israel to be a people unto thee for ever: and thou, LORD, art become their God"* (II Samuel 7:23-24).

The origin of the races has been a subject of great interest among many people, especially those whose instincts and intelligence confirm the tremendous physical, psychological, mental, biological, and spiritual differences that separate the various races of the earth. While the subject of anthropology is a branch of learning that encompasses a broad range of knowledge, it will not greatly influence this study. The single aim of this short essay is to inquire into what the Bible, the Holy Word of God, has to say about the origin of the races. We are not concerned here with the vast number of university professors, research papers, books, and self-styled experts on the subject of race. **We simply want to know what the Bible has to say about race. Where did the separate races come from?**

EXPOSING ERROR IN THE CHURCH

The 20th century Church, few denominations excepted, is largely responsible for much of the misinformation circulating on this subject. The Church has followed the world in making gross assumptions about the origin of the races, and more particularly, the Church is guilty of making outrageous claims upon the Word regarding this subject which cannot be defended from the Bible. You can search the Bible forever without being able to validate what 20th century Christians believe about race. Before opening the pages of the Bible to ascertain what Scripture does say, let us challenge error currently being taught in the church.

ALL RACES DESCENDED FROM ADAM

The 20th century Christian world, almost without exception, teaches a common origin of all races--Caucasian, Oriental, and Negroid--in Adam. Most confess that the variations of brown, mulatto, etc... result from miscegenation of these three races. However, most theologians refuse to acknowledge whether Adam was created Caucasian, Mongoloid, or Negroid. For most Christians, it makes little difference whether Adam was created white, yellow, black, or any other hue. For them, the words *mankind, human being, and homo sapiens* describe all of humanity. When they turn to Genesis 1:26 and read about the creation of man, they interpret Adam as a universal man and fail to consider whether he is white, yellow, or black; it makes little difference to them, for from this one man Adam, *Jehovah* made all races of the earth. **Sincere Christians, however, reject this premise for the following reasons.**

RANK EVOLUTION

The belief that all races descended from Adam is rank evolution, a theory that expounds from many (almost all!) pulpits in the land. To really believe that the biological, psychological, mental, physical, and spiritual diversity in the races results from a common beginning is gross heresy. No Christian can buy this outrageous and unscriptural teaching. Every effort to prove a unity of beginning has met dismal failure. All the scientific research and study has never confirmed one minute bit of evidence to support that all races descended from one set of parents. **What faith it would take to believe that Adam and Eve are the parents of all races!**

When one places racial differences under the microscope, the radical diversity is amazing. Skin color is only the beginning. Blood composition is entirely different. Lung capacity is different. Brain weight and convolution vary greatly. Mental and spiritual values are radically different. Fertility factors vary. Inward and spiritual instincts are different. Some races are nocturnal, while others are not. Innate religious drives are different. Diseases of the blood vary from one race to another and can be peculiar to one race. Motor qualities vary from one race to the another. Hair and eye color patterns vary radically. The more closely one observes the races, the more glaring the differences become. **To believe that all of these evolved from one common beginning is ludicrous, alien to all common sense.**

ERROR IN THE CHVRCH

A majority of all Christians and most churches that still revere the Bible believe that the Genesis flood left only Noah, his wife, and three sons--Shem, Ham, and Japheth--and their wives, on the earth. Denominational ministers, assuming that the Genesis flood left only Noah and his family alive on earth, have scrambled to establish theological grounds for the existence of different races following the Genesis flood. A large majority of them teach that all races on earth descended from Noah's three sons. They claim that the Negroid race descended from Ham, the Mongoloid race from Japheth, and the Caucasian race from Shem. This has become the premise upon which most Christians rest their case. Again, a common unity of race in Noah is their thesis. **Sincere Christians reject this premise because it is rank evolution. To believe that all the distinct races on earth are descended from Noah and his sons is an insult to *Jehovah*, His Word, and the physical and spiritual laws of the universe.**

MORE ERROR IN THE CHVRCH

Teaching a racial unity in Adam and Noah has allowed 20th century theologians and their followers to discard the basic laws of the Holy Bible. The Law of Kind after His Kind, established ten times in Genesis 1, has been trashed. The Bible teaching of segregation, separation, and racial purity has been thrown to the winds. The Scriptural meaning of *Adam man* has been totally ignored. The major thesis of the Bible itself has been lost amid the rubble of evolutionary humanism. Moreover, most theologians and their followers, stand on their heads trying to prove race mixing is permissible in Scripture. There seems to be a mania to mix, mate, and amalgamate in the modern Church. Interracial marriage, once disdained and forbidden in the

Church, is now openly encouraged. Both the pulpit and the pew of the modern Church are dead set on miscegenation. Because the Church teaches a unity of all races in Adam and Noah, this evolutionary humanism has laid the foundation for race mixing on a scale never known in the history of the Western world.

BIBLE TRUTH ABOUT RACE

What does the Bible teach about the origin of the races? Since the Bible is the source of all truth for the Christian, this is an important question. There can be no truth or knowledge apart from God and His Word. Scripture is the reference point for all knowledge, and the subject of race is no exception. The following postulates, while not pleasing to many, are necessary in arriving at truth. If you are a seeker of the truth and are open to reflect upon such important matters as the origin of the races, then the following discussion may be helpful for you. If you have already set your thinking in stone and are closed to possibility thinking, the following presuppositions will be excused and forgotten.

THE BIBLE IS AN EXCLUSIVE BOOK

The Bible was not written for all the races of the earth. Just as the Koran speaks to the Moslem mind, the Talmud speaks to the Jewish psyche, the Veda fills the Hindu need for spirituality, Voodoo meets the spiritual needs of the Negroid, and Confucius appeals to the Oriental mind, the Bible has historically fulfilled the spiritual needs of the Caucasian race. While most all races have their plethora of gods, including Allah, Brahman, Confucius, Baal, Dagon, and others, **Jesus Christ is the Savior of the Caucasian Christian faith!** Regardless of cultural and language differences, Caucasians historically have been linked to the

Christian faith. Like most religious works, the Bible clearly defines who it is written to, for, and about.

Genesis 5:1-3 declares: *"This is the book of the genera-tions of Adam. In the day that God created man, In the likeness of God made he him; Male and female created he them; and blessed them, and called their name Adam, in the day when they were created."* **The Bible is the history and record of one race of people: Adam. After Genesis 12, the Bible confines itself primarily to the study of one branch of the Adamic race, the line of Shem, Eber (Hebrew), Isaac, and Jacob Israel. The Bible never claims to be the history of all races. Not one verse can be used to support any idea that the Bible is the universal history and chronicle of all the races under heaven.**

Plainly in Genesis 5:1-3, the Bible claims to be the record of Adam kind. These verses emphatically tie together the man of Genesis 1:26-28, Genesis 2:7, and Genesis 2:24-25 so that we are not talking about two creations in Genesis 1 and 2. The Bible is the record of one race--Adam. Gen-esis 1:26-27 talks about the creation of the incorporeal soul of Adam man, not his body. His body is created in Genesis 2:7. His soul does not become living, that is, it does not have self-consciousness, until that soul is placed within the body at creation. It is at conception that the spirit is breathed into the body to give it life and con-sciousness to the soul. Genesis 1 and 2 both refer to Adam man. There is no Biblical grounds for teaching two cre-ations in Genesis 1 and 2, one Pre-Adamic and the other Adamic. The word *man* in Genesis 1:26 comes from the same Hebrew root word as Genesis 2:7, #120 (*Aw-Dawm*), Adam, meaning ruddy, a human being, an individual or the species, mankind.

In summary, the Bible is generally the record of Adam kind, and the Hebrew-Israel branch of the Adamic creation in particular. Moreover, a careful study of the Hebrew meaning of the word *Adam* confirms that Adam was the first Caucasian, the first white man, to stand on the earth. The Bible, then, is the history of the Caucasian race, not any other. It is true that the Bible will discuss other races, but only as they involve the story of Adam man. The Bible never makes a point of becoming the history of another race. Its primary focus is the study of Israel, a branch of the Adamic race. Particularly, it is the story of Abraham's family, through his son Isaac, grandson Jacob-Israel, and the twelve tribes descending from him. There are no genealogical tables giving the history of the Egyptians, Chinese, Hindus, Japanese, Negroid, and others because the Bible is the history of the Adamic race in general, and Israel in particular.

If you were to build a family history of your people, you would not expect to find the names and history of all the people in the city in which you live. You might include the name of an occasional close neighbor, but your history would be confined to your people. Such is the Bible. It is the story of Adam in the early chapters of Genesis, and then of Abraham and his family, the Israelites in particular, from Genesis 12 through the remainder of the New Testament. If you were to buy a new Ford, you would expect your owner's manual to tell you all about a Ford. You would never expect to find information about the Buick your neighbor is driving in your Ford manual. Such is the Bible. If you are looking for the history of Mongoloid or Negroid race, or even the specific genealogies of the Caucasian race, forget it. The Bible is the record of the Adamic people, and in particular, the Caucasian branch known as the Israelites.

THE CHAY NEFFESH CREATION

The question might arise as to how the other races fit into the scheme of creation. Without being dogmatic, if the Bible includes the record of how the non-Adamic races were created, it is found in Genesis 1:25 where the *Chay Neffesh* creation, or living creatures, are named. The living creatures here could have been biped as well as quadruped. It was not the purpose of the Creator to particularize the creation of other races. We know that *Jehovah* is the creator of all things in heaven and earth; everything He created was pronounced good (Genesis 1:31). The *Chay Neffesh* creation, if it does include other races, means that they were created by *Jehovah* and found to be good, perfect, in His creative work.

Remember that every race bears the original design of the Creator. Skin color, blood composition, skeletal differences, brain convolutions, and vast numbers of other racial differences all are distinctive marks of God's ownership on every race. Every race was created good, unique, and gifted to fulfill its particular function in the creation. Every race can know and communicate with the Creator, but each in a different way. No one dare remove the mark of God's ownership on every race by miscegenation. Race mixing destroys the original design of every race and makes a mockery of God and His eternal Law.

The worth of every race is important to the total purpose and plan of the great Creator of heaven and earth. Every race bears precisely what God purposed for it to bring forth in the life chain of creation. What must be carefully considered are both value and function of the race in question. All are important in God's plan. Representative members of all the races will be in His Kingdom, but standing in different function and position. While representatives of all the created races in their original and pure state will pass into the

Kingdom through natural generation, the saved members of Adam kind will enter the Kingdom through translation or resurrection.

Every race has a definitive function to fill in the Creator's great plan for His earth, and no man dares to diminish the work of the Master Potter. Only through careful maintenance of racial purity can every race retain the original design given them by the Creator. Moreover, racial purity and segregation is the only valid way that the innate gifts, talents, and blessings of every race will be preserved. The Adamic creation was given the dominion mandate (Genesis 1:28, 2:15), and all other races were assigned a function in the plan and purpose of the Creator. No race will be satisfied and blessed when forced to serve outside that function for which they were created. You cannot force a Negroid into a function designed for Adam man. You cannot place a Caucasian in the role of a Negroid. The Bible plan of segregation insures the racial purity of every race, preserving its original design and blessing.

ADAM KIND CREATION

In the Genesis account of creation, Adam man is the particularized creation. While *Jehovah* obviously created other races separately, the Bible makes no effort to detail this creation because it was not intended to be the family history of any race other than Adam kind. We know that God created all life forms in the animal world; yet they are not specifically listed in the Genesis account of creation. It is understood that God Almighty created all life forms in the ocean, but the whale is the only life form that is specifically named. The fact that Adam man is the only biped creature named in the Genesis account of creation does not mean that other races were not created. All races were created by *Jehovah*, and they fall into the Living Creature classification of Genesis 1:24-25. The Bible record does not give any specific or detailed account for the non-Adamic races because this is not the record of their family history. They were created very good (Genesis 1:31) and have a function to fill in His world. Beyond this the Bible is silent on the development of the other races.

A FAMILY HISTORY

When you open the Bible, you are reading the family history of one race of people, Adam kind. Specifically, you read from Genesis 12 forward of the history of Abraham and his family through his son Isaac and grandson Jacob. The Bible is really an Israelite book. It was written over a period of some sixteen hundred years by Israelites who were separated by great expanses of time, and sometimes distance. From the first book, Genesis, to the last book, the Revelation Letter of Jesus Christ, the Bible is a family history written to, for, and about Israel. He that hath ears to hear, let him hear.

10

WHITE SEPARATISM

A CHRISTIAN AND BIBLICAL VISION FOR OUR TIME IN HISTORY

"For wherein shall it be known here that I and thy people have found grace in thy sight? Is it not in that thou goest with us? so shall we be separated, I and thy people, from all the people that are upon the face of the earth." "And ye shall be holy unto me: for I the LORD *am holy, and have severed you from other people, that ye should be mine" (Exodus 33:16, Leviticus 20:26).*

There is urgent need for a vision in our time of history, for without it, the people will perish (Proverbs 29:18). Millions of Caucasian people are adrift upon the sea of life without a vision, and having no spiritual compass or north star to guide them, they are truly lost. These lost sheep move from one church to another, seeking to find the answer to their spiritual needs. Most of them seek in vain to find that spiritual vision that will meet their need for spiritual and physical preservation. Living at the end of the Western Christian culture, specifically in its death phase, it will not be easy to find a lighthouse amid the perilous waves that wash over our lives. There is one lasting hope as we find salvation by faith in Jesus Christ, repent from dead works, and seek to live on the High Road of Christian and Biblical truth. That hope is to move forward with the vision of Biblical **separatism.** The preservation of the spiritual and physical lives of a Christian remnant is the highest priority of our time.

Those people who desire to walk in the Christian and Biblical truth of their God must make a choice in favor of the only valid option open to the Christian remnant. Biblical separatism is the only door through which the Christian, Caucasian remnant may find hope in this time of Jacob's Trouble. The covenant people of Scripture dare not integrate, amalgamate, and yoke themselves with mainstream American and survive. White separatism demands full secession from the Christian-Judeo religious world, geographical separation from the mixed multitude, and total separation from the moral standards of this generation. Either we separate ourselves from sin, or sin will separate us from God. Our children simply cannot survive spiritually, morally, and physically without separation. Segregation, not **integration,** is the call of God to the covenant people of this generation.

Without a vision, the people will perish (Proverbs 29:18), and without a vision of white, Christian separatism, our children have no future in this country. The complete religious, social, biological, and moral integration and fusion of America demands that Christian people act with all dispatch and follow the footsteps of their ancestors and the clear call of Scripture to practice separatism. The Pilgrim and Puritan fathers who settled and sparked the beginning of the United States of America were religious separatists seeking a place where they could preserve and practice their spiritual priorities. The spiritual priorities of Israelites living in the United States of America can be achieved only through religious, racial, and moral separation from mainstream America. Those who remain inexorably integrated into contemporary American culture and life may want to read about Lot and the city of Sodom and Gomorrah to find out what their end will be.

Inherent within every race is the tendency toward separatism, and one can find evidence of separatism being practiced by members of the black and yellow races, Hispanics, Jews, and other racial and ethnic groups. This tendency is confirmation of the basic Law of Kind after Its Kind enumerated ten times in the first chapter of Genesis. By the original design of God there is a genetic tendency for every race to practice separatism. God and Scripture segregate, while man and the religion of humanism tend to integrate. Separatism is a law that is basic to God and the Creation. Plants reproduce according to the Law of Kind after Its Kind and Seed in Itself. Birds of a feather flock together: blackbirds feed, cluster, and travel with other blackbirds. The animals of the forest reproduce and establish social habits according to these basic laws. All of God's creation demonstrate the spiritual and biological law of separatism. It is unnatural, unscriptural, and in violation of the harmony of creation to integrate, amalgamate, and bring about a fusion of the separate races which God, our Creator, placed in this earth.

One merely has to examine the ethnic clustering of people within the boundaries of the Soviet Union, Eastern Europe, and elsewhere to validate that people have a natural proclivity to practice and live by the law of separatism. The Amish and Mennonite communities in America have practiced separatism since their arrival in this country. The Jewish people have practiced racial separatism throughout their history. Many blacks tend to favor separatism. It has required the force of Federal and State legislation, Federal and State court decrees, and one full generation of pressure from the pulpits and university chairs, to bring about the racial integration of American society, and there continues to remain evidence of racial and ethnic separatism within the 250 million people constituting the American population base. It is not difficult to find definite clustering of Chinese, Hispanics, Negroes, Japanese, Vietnamese, Arabian, and other racial and ethnic groups within contemporary America. The racial and religious integration of American society is far from being realized, despite the force of government, church, and social pressure. White flight to the American suburbs is a typical, innate response to the genetic law of racial segregation that continues to operate in the Caucasian mind.

The survival of every distinct racial and ethnic group is dependent upon the practice of separatism. Every racial group in the United States of America must be free to practice this. Racial separatism is also practiced within the various ethnic groupings of the Caucasian race, and rightly so. While vast numbers, indeed the majority of whites, have elected to integrate racially, religiously, socially, and morally with members of all other races, there remains a large remnant within the Caucasian community and every other racial group (including Jews, blacks, and Orientals) who practice some form of racial and ethnic separatism.

The call must go forth for the Christian remnant to covenant, combine, and separate themselves into spiritual, moral, and racial enclaves. These people must be willing to work together for the mutual survival of their children and their way of life. Caucasian Christians who fail to practice separatism among their own spiritual and racial kind will be making the major mistake of their lives. They and their children, for all time to come, will regret having failed to move forward with the vision of ethnic separatism.

The focus of the entire Israelite community living in the United States of America and other Israelite nations abroad should give careful consideration to this spiritual vision. We must move forward with a vision of white separatism if we are to survive as the covenant people of God in this earth. Following the pattern of the Amish and Mennonites, Jews and Chinese, Arabs and inner city blacks, Israelites must practice white separatism.

White separatism must be practiced within the rural landscape of America and other Israelite nations including the Dominion of Canada, the British Isles, Scandinavia, Europe, Australia, S. Africa, New Zealand and elsewhere in this earth. Failure of the fathers and pastors to set a vision of white separatism before our people will have horrible consequences in the years to come. Time is of the essence. With all dispatch the fathers and pastors of the Israelite remnant must move forward to plant the vision of white separatism and establish Christian Covenant Settlements throughout the rural landscape of America.

The idea of separatism is not new to America. There are population concentrations within every racial group living in America who exhibit some form of racial exclusiveness. White separatism is innovative because historically, America has been a white man's country. Now that the Caucasian race is becoming the minority race, it is natural for groups within it to do what other racial and ethnic peoples have been doing for some time, and that is practice racial and religious separatism. In planting white Christian settlements in the rural sectors of the United States and other Israelite nations of the Western world, the long term survival of these people can be assured.

If racial separatism can be practiced by all other races living in the United States, the white race of this country ought to enjoy this blessing under the protection of the United States Constitution and the respective state constitutions where these people live. White separatism calls for the peaceful and orderly settlement of Caucasian Christian people in sparsely populated rural areas of America. The goal of these people will be to organize themselves upon the land, worship *Jehovah* in spirit and truth, keep and follow His commandments, work the land and shops, home school their children, and live in peace among themselves and the communities where they reside.

These settlements should work hard to avoid tension or hostility with the existing population. There should be no cause for friction or hostility with the existing population. Areas of low density white rural population centers will be expressly sought out to avoid hostility. These Christian Covenant Settlements should establish high moral standards so that they will attract people of the highest rank of Godliness, honesty, and morality. All forms of agriculture and animal husbandry, home cottage industry, and other honest business enterprises will become the primary economic base for the sustenance of these people. Their primary focus will be to worship and serve Jesus Christ, to live and serve one another, and to preserve the spiritual and racial heritage of their children in this country.

Those in the Christian remnant who reside in these rural settlements know they are living in the time of Jacob's trouble (Jeremiah 30:7), a time where there is great pain and suffering among the people. Moreover, these people realize that it is important to practice repentance and walk in fear and trembling before *Jehovah*. They perceive that the non-white races now pouring upon America are here as a judgment. They do not view the arrival of the third world aliens as a cause for conflict and war. The swarming of third-world people upon the American Fatherland results from the sin and wickedness of the white population which has long since broken covenant with God and His immutable Law. White separatism seeks to bring together a remnant of the Israelite people in the rural areas where they can live peacefully under Jesus Christ and the Holy Scriptures.

If most of the white population desires to integrate, amalgamate, and worship heathen gods and idols, they must know that there is a remnant who has made a different choice. There is a God-fearing, Bible-believing, sin-hating, blood-washed, spirit-filled Israelite remnant living in the United States of America who has made the choice to worship and serve God, to follow His commandments, and preserve the racial and spiritual heritage of their children upon the soil of the American fatherland. Their religious conscience forbids them from integrating their spiritual and racial values with the liberal humanism of the contemporary American mindset.

SCRIPTURAL PROOFS FOR WHITE SEPARATISM

The Holy Bible builds a powerful case in favor of white separatism. Hear what we read in the great discourse between Yahweh and Moses in Exodus 33:16: *"For wherein shall it be known here that I and thy people have found grace in thy sight? is it not in that thou goest with us? so shall we be separated, I and thy people, from all the people that are upon the face of the earth."* Scholarship confirms that the Israelites of the Bible were called to be a separated people unto *Jehovah*. The doctrine of separatism was established from the beginning by divine decree. In Leviticus 20:24, Israel is reminded by *Jehovah* that they have been separated from other people. Leviticus 20:26 says, *"And ye shall be holy unto me: for I the Lord am holy, and have severed you from other people, that ye should be mine.*" In the very first blessing which Balaam pronounced upon Israel, he declared that Israel was to **dwell alone** and not be reckoned among the nations (Numbers 23:9--emphasis ours). In Deuteronomy 7:2-3, the Israelites were forbidden to make any covenant with the heathen people, and they were expressly forbidden to allow their sons or daughters to marry anyone from these nations. Joshua 23:7 records that the Israelites were not to associate with the heathen non-Israelite nations, that they were to have no social activity with these people and were to abstain from the worship of all heathen gods.

That the God of Scripture determined to separate His people Israel from the rest of the nations of the earth is confirmed in the Song of Moses as recorded in Deuteronomy 32:8-9: *"When the Most High divided to the nations their inheritance, when he separated the sons of Adam, he set the bounds of the people according to the number of the children of Israel. For the LORD's portion is his people; Jacob is the lot of his inheritance."* This is further confirmed in Solomon's dedication prayer of the great temple in I Kings 8:53. *"For thou didst separate them (Israel) from among all the people of the earth, to be thine inheritance, as thou sparest by the hand of Moses thy servant, when thou brightest our fathers out of Egypt, O Lord God."*

Biblical Israel was given careful instruction from the beginning to abstain from interracial marriage with the heathen nations surrounding them. One of the primary benefits of the doctrine of separatism is protection from the consequences of interracial marriage. This is emphasized in Ezra 9:12 where Israelites were forbidden to engage in interracial marriage with the people of the lands where they dwelt: *"Now therefore give not your daughters unto their sons, neither take their daughters unto your sons, not seek their peace or their wealth for ever: that ye may be strong, and eat the good of the land, and leave it for an inheritance to your children for ever."* Under the leadership of Ezra, the Israelites who had intermarried with non-Israelite people were required to separate. *"Now therefore make confession unto the LORD God of your fathers, and do his pleasure: and separate yourselves from the people of the land, and from the strange wives"* (Ezra 10:11). Nehemiah 13:3 is further confirmation of the importance of separatism among the Israelites. *"Now it came to pass, when they had heard the law, that they separated from Israel all the mixed multitude."*

On occasion, the Israelites were forced to establish themselves in covenant settlements where they could preserve the spiritual and racial standards of Scripture and remain a separated people unto *Jehovah*. This is graphically described in Nehemiah 10.

"And the rest of the people, the priests, the Levites, the porters, the singers, the Nethinims, and all they that had separated themselves from the people of the lands unto the law of God, their wives, their sons, and their daughters, every one having knowledge, and having understanding; They clave to their brethren, their nobles, and entered into a curse, and into an oath, to walk in God's law, which was given by Moses the servant of God, and to observe and do all the commandments of the LORD our Lord, and his judgments and his statutes; And that we would not give our daughters unto the people of the land, nor take their daughters for our sons."

The Israelite remnant living in the United States of America, the Dominion of Canada, the British Isles, Scandinavia, Europe, South Africa, Australia and elsewhere on this planet has no option but to separate and then covenant together in Christian settlements where they can pre-serve the spiritual and racial standards of the Law of *Jeho-vah* for themselves and their children. All of the Israelite nations of the Western world were racially separated from the rest of the world until the 20th century. The racial com-position of all the major Israelite nations is undergoing powerful change. With this change there is a total culture displacement. The art, literature, music, language, and en-tertainment of the Western world are taking on the stan-dards of the non-white world. Israelite parents have no choice but to remove their children from this life-threaten-ing mixed multitude. Israelite parents must take their chil-dren, regroup in the rural areas of the United States and other Israelite nations, and return to the perfect Law of *Jehovah* as the only standard by which we and our chil-dren can live.

The settlement of these families in the rural enclaves of America is something that is already taking place. How-ever, the pace of this movement must be accelerated in view of the gathering world storm. Israelite families need to clus-ter in these rural areas all across America, buy small and large farmsteads, establish a Church, and practice free market enterprise among themselves and the indigenous population. **We are not talking about communal living!** We refer to privately owned farmsteads, truck farms, and cattle and sheep ranches, orchards, and cottage industries where our people can become economically self-sustaining in coming days of tribulation. The long range forecast for the economic welfare of America is not good. We must work to become as self-sufficient as possible we are able to sur-vive the recession/depression cycles of America along with the plunging standard of living. The ability to produce our own energy, grow our own food, produce our own clothing, and become generally self-sufficient will be imperative in the days that are unfolding.

These Israelite settlements should be scattered throughout rural America with care given to the better growing seasons, more favorable climate, and low density population, industry, and defense centers. Long range weather forecasts indicate a cooling trend; consequently, the growing season in the northern regions of the country may be cut short. Avoid large concentrations of people in these settlements. These settlements should be widely distributed over America, north and south, east and west. Great care should be given to the establishment of a strong, Christ-centered, Bible-based Church that is faithful to the Commandments of *Jehovah* and where the people seek to live with a spiritual focus of serving God and one another. Faithful obedience to the weekly Sabbath and annual festivals of the Bible is important to the long range survival of these settlements.

The time has come for kingdom pastors, fathers, and grand-fathers to awaken from our lukewarm positions and take all the necessary steps to encourage Israelite parents and their children to enter a time of serious commitment with Jesus Christ, restore ourselves under Bible Law, and cluster together in covenant Church settlements throughout America. The steps that we take today will insure the preservation of our children tomorrow. This is the day for white separatism to be preached and practiced among Israelite people. Separatism is taking place among all the other racial and ethnic groups living in America. When will the covenant people of the Bible, the Anglo-Saxon, Celtic, Germanic, Scandinavian, and kindred people of America and Israelite nations abroad awaken to the need to preserve a people pure and undefiled for the second coming of Jesus Christ? Israelites, stop, think, look, and listen to the call of the Holy Spirit! **Spiritual and racial separatism is the only solution to the mixed multitude now gathering in our land.**

11

THE SIN OF MISCEGENATION

"And the children of Israel dwelt among the Canaanites, Hittites, and Amorites, and Perizzites, and Hivites, and Jebusites: And they took their daughters to be their wives, and gave their daughters to their sons, and served their gods. And the children of Israel did evil in the sight of the LORD, and forgot the LORD their God, and served Baalim and the groves" (Judges 3:5-7).

A terrible and unforgivable sin is being carried forth in the United States of America and the Israelite nations of the Western world. Caucasian Israelite people are marrying and mixing with non-white third world aliens from Africa, Asia, India, Mexico, and far flung heathen nations of the world. The moral crime of miscegenation is openly encouraged and promoted by many of the 450,000 ministers in America. The Church has found the sin of miscegenation to be acceptable doctrine, and its doors are opened wide to race mixing of every kind. Ministers of every denominational stripe welcome black and white couples, white and yellow, and white and brown couples before the altar where marriages are solemnized in the name of Jesus Christ.

The government--at every level of operation, following the desires of the people and encouraged by thousands of ministers--has legislated the moral crime of miscegenation into statutory law in the United States of America. Race mixing is now openly flaunted with the approval of the Churches and is protected under legislation passed by the Federal and State legislative bodies. Without compunction, millions of fathers and mothers allow their sons and daughters to socialize and attend classes with, worship with, date, and marry Asians, Negroids, Mexicans and other non-whites. America is now the home of thousands of interracially mixed couples; tens of thousands of bastard (mongrel) children swell the population of this land.

The sin of miscegenation is now a scourge throughout our land. Pressure from the churches, the news media, Hollywood film producers, the public schools, and the ever-growing presence of non-white, third world aliens have accelerated the moral sin of race mixing beyond human calculation. Blood pollution covers our land. The blood of the Anglo-Saxon, Germanic, world is being squandered upon the godless, Satanic altar of miscegenation. This baneful sin is now legalized under color of law in America. While race-mixing may be *legal* (man made legislation), it is not *lawful* (as per God's immutable law). Miscegenation is a moral crime that reaches to heaven, is repugnant to all Christians, and is rank blasphemy in the eyes of God. The presence of race-mixing in American society sears the conscience of all true Christians and threatens the very future of the American fatherland. No nation in all of human history has ever survived the scourge of miscegenation. When the blood of Caucasian-Israel is mixed with other races, the end of civilization is at hand.

As confirmed in the Gospel of St. Luke 17:22-30, Jesus Christ points out that miscegenation (race-mixing) and sodomy (male homosexuality) would characterize the age of history that would witness His Second Coming in power and glory. The crimes of miscegenation and sodomy are now accelerating at a level never known in all of human history. Wholesale race mixing is now taking place in America and most of the Israelite nations of the earth. Sodomy is a moral crime that threatens the spiritual fabric of American society. It is high time the Church of the Living God take a strong Scriptural stand on both of these moral battlefronts.

The Holy Bible condemns the crime of miscegenation from one cover to another. There is no place in God's Word for the sin of race mixing. We can summarize why miscegenation is an affront to Almighty God and His Word with the following affirmations of truth: firstly, race mixing destroys the original design that the Creator purposed for every race. Every race was created separately and distinctly. Miscegenation seeks to erase God's special mark of ownership upon every race and defy the very intelligence and wisdom of a Sovereign God. Secondly, miscegenation is a violation of the Law of Kind after Its Kind, which appears no less than ten times in the creation chapter of Genesis one. The Law of Kind after Its Kind demands the racial purity of every race. Miscegenation assaults the purity of every race and is a rank violation of God's immutable law.

Thirdly, race mixing violates the Law of Seed in Itself enumerated in Genesis 1:11. Every race, created separately and distinctly, has its own inherent, genetic blueprint locked in the genes. Miscegenation scrambles these genes and violates the Law of Seed in Itself. Fourthly, mixing of the races is condemned by every law of God that operates within the natural world of plants, animals, and birds. Miscegenation is unknown among plants, animals, and birds. White birds and black birds never mix. The cardinal has remained fixed in his genes from the dawn of creation. The zebra, when left in his natural state, will not mate with the horse. Only when man seeks to circumvent the immutable laws of God and elevate human reason above the wisdom of God in forced interbreeding does miscegenation ever occur within the creation of plants, animals, birds, and fishes. The mule would become extinct without the artificial forcing of the donkey and the horse. God's Word does not lie! Race mixing is wrong, and those nations which allow such moral reprobation will be judged by the wrath of an angry God.

Fifthly, miscegenation represents an assault upon the Holy Scripture. Nowhere in the Holy Bible does God provide for the mixing of the races. The Bible presents *Jehovah* as a God of segregation and separation. The idea of racial amalgamation is foreign to every moral fibre taught in God's Holy Word. Sixthly, the sin of race mixing represents the final stage in the breaking of God's Law. Miscegenation is the last stage of moral reprobation. When the blood of the Caucasian and the Negroid (or any other different races) mix, the point of no return has been reached. Once the blood is polluted, it is done forever.

Finally, miscegenation denies the record of six thousand years of human history. No people engaged in race mixing ever survived. History is strewn with the great nations that were dissolved into chaos and ruin when they openly courted and encouraged race mixing. Let us now turn to some salient Scriptures in the Bible to confirm the terrible nature of race mixing.

THE BIBLE RECORD AGAINST MISCEGENATION

The great deluge of Noah's generation was precipitated by the sin of miscegenation. The record of Genesis six confirms that out-of-kind marriages ended in the judgment of a flood upon that wicked and apostate generation. Only Noah and his household were found racially and morally pure then. That all flesh had corrupted its way is the testimony of Genesis 6:12. That corruption involved out-of-kind marriages. Jesus Christ confirmed this to be true in St. Matthew 24:37-39 and St. Luke 17:26-29. That the sin of race mixing would characterize the ending of this age is revealed in St. Matthew 24:22 wherein Jesus Christ declared that *"except those days should be short-ened, there should no flesh be saved: but for the elect's sake, those days shall be shortened"* (Jeremiah 31:27). This confirms that the House of Israel would move into total racial and moral reprobation by first mixing with the seed of Adam and finally with the seed of the beast. The plain truth is that Jeremiah 31:27 is now being confirmed in the streets, sidewalks, market places, and churches of the western world.

The call of Abraham and the development of the cov-enant seedline in history is clear confirmation of *Jehovah*'s plan for the racial purity of His people. Abraham married his half sister Sarah to produce a certified seedline for the subsequent purpose of God in the unfolding of history (Genesis 20:12). The selection of Isaac to be heir to the Abrahamic covenant is a major topic of the Genesis record. The mating of Isaac with a woman of his own covenant family is the theme of Genesis 24. Genesis 27:46 and 28:1 validate the plan of Isaac and Rebekah to find a wife for Jacob among their own people. Jacob's marriages to Leah and Rachel are carefully chronicled in Scripture. Selective breeding within the covenant family is confirmed in the narrative of the Holy Bible. There is no room in God's plan for race mixing. The preservation of a holy seed is a major occupation of the purpose of God in the history of His people Israel.

The Israelite occupation of the land of Goshen in Egypt was *Jehovah*'s plan for keeping His people separated from the Egyptians. The Israelites multiplied in Egypt, preserved their own racial identity and moral and spiritual customs, and failed to be integrated into Egyptian society after several generations of close contact. When the Israelites left Egypt, a mixed multitude or racial rabble followed them out; but this racially mixed rabble was never acceptable with *Jehovah*. Numbers 11:4 reveals that this mixed multitude led Israel into lusting. Its presence might have been the reason for the injunction given in Exodus 19:13 that not a hand of beast or of man touch the holy mount. The hand of beast in this scripture would be referring to someone other than an Israelite.

In the development of Israel's Divine Service of Worship, *Jehovah* mandated that corporate worship be segregated. In Exodus 12:47, all the congregation of Israel were to keep the Passover. The foreigner and the hired servant were not to eat of the Passover (Exodus 12:45). Only Israelite males were required to appear three times yearly at the appointed festivals (Exodus 23:17 and Deut. 16:16). Only Israelites--men, women, and children--were to assemble for the appointed festivals (Deut. 31:9-13). The weekly Sabbath was an exclusive sign that marked Israel as the people of *Jehovah* (Exodus 31:12-17). Deuteronomy 23:2 confirms that bastards (mamzers, racial mongrels) were not permitted into the congregation of the Eternal even unto the tenth generation. The Lamentations of Jeremiah 1:10 reveal that unauthorized heathen had entered the Sanctuary. The Biblical injunction against integrated worship services is also established in Ezekiel 44:7.

The Bible record is replete with examples of how Israelites came under judgment as a result of the sin of miscegenation (Leviticus 24:10-16). In this instance an Israelite woman named Shelomith of the tribe of Dan married an Egyptian man. The son born to this unlawful marriage committed blasphemy unto *Jehovah* and was later put to death. The divine injunction against the integration of Israel with other races is clearly established in Deuteronomy 7:2-3 where the Israelites were not only warned against making covenants with non-Israelite people, but also were expressly warned against marriages with these people. Numbers 36:6 confirms that Israelite women were not only to marry only Israelites, but also were to marry within the tribe of their father. The Holy Scriptures condemn race mixing as a clear violation of God's eternal law.

The Biblical case against miscegenation is clearly revealed in Numbers 25:1-18 wherein the Israelite males began to commit whoredom with the daughters of Moab. By this time in history (B.C. 1452), the Moabites had mongrelized themselves with a variety of heathen peoples. Wholesale race mixing with the Moabites not only resulted in the pollution of the Israelite bloodline, but also brought Israelites into idolatry. The Israelites were beginning to worship Baal, a Moabite deity associated with Mt. Peor. The worship of Baalpeor and race mixing with the Moabite women caused the wrath of God to wax hot against Israel. This miscegenation was viewed with great alarm by the leadership in Israel and by the God of Scripture; those guilty were dealt serious punishment.

The case of Zimri and Cozbi in Numbers 24:6-18 validates the Biblical case against miscegenation. In this instance, an Israelite man named Zimri, a chief man of the tribe of Simeon, had joined himself with Cozbi, the daughter of Zur, a chief man of the Midianites. By this time the Midianites had corrupted themselves by mingling with diverse people over a period of many generations. When Zimri brought the Midianitish woman into the sanctuary and displayed his race mixing desires before all Israel, Phinehas, son of Aaron, rose up, took a javelin, and ended the lives of both Zimri and Cozbi. Phinehas was steward over the Sanctuary. As an authority figure in the Sanctuary and in the priesthood, he was responsible for keeping the tabernacle of the congregation holy unto *Jehovah*. Because of his action, the plague was stayed from Israel, and Yahweh entered a covenant that called for an everlasting priesthood with Phinehas and his seed after him.

The Book of Judges establishes the Bible case against miscegenation. In this instance, the Israelites were involving themselves with interracial marriages with the Canaanite nations around them. This process of miscegenation not only brought strong rebuke for the mixed marriages, but also for the practice of idolatry, which always follows the sin of race-mixing.

The case against miscegenation in the Holy Scriptures is further outlined in the many Biblical injunctions prescribed for moral purity of the Israelites. Consider that in Leviticus 18 and 20 and in numerous other areas of Scripture, Israelites were forbidden to practice incest, adultery, sodomy, and miscegenation. Leviticus 20:15 and 16 include a prohibition against physical intimacy with the living creatures as outlined in Genesis 1:24 and 25. The physical intimacy of the Israelites was insulated not only against every form of incest, adultery, fornication, sodomy, prostitution, and miscegenation, but also from violations within the marriage covenant. Leviticus 15:1-13 governs the control and cure of infectious venereal disease, and Leviticus 15:19, 18:19, and 20:18 govern restrictions on physical intimacy during the menstrual cycle. *Jehovah* purposed to hedge the Israelites with very strong moral laws which included the injunction against every form of interracial marriage.

Jeremiah the Prophet pronounced the wrath of God upon Judah because of the sin of miscegenation (Jeremiah 2:21-

22). In this instance, the prophet reminds the people that much washing with soap cannot remove the iniquity of race mixing. In Malachi 2:11-12, Judah is again brought into accountability for interracial marriage with the heathen. The Prophet Malachi warns that those who enter into these unlawful marriages will be cut off from *Jehovah*.

In Ezra 9:1-15 and 10:1-9, the Bible confirms a strong case against the sin of miscegenation. When Ezra the Priest-Scribe returned from the Babylonian captivity and entered Jerusalem, he witnessed the scourge of miscegenation. Ezra 9 is the heart-rending appeal which he makes to God for this and other moral sins committed against *Jehovah*. Ezra 10:18-19 outlines the fact that those who entered marriages with non-Israelites did put away these strange wives. In Nehemiah 9:1-2, the Israelites confessed the sin of miscegenation, and in Nehemiah 10:28-30, they covenanted that they would not allow the sons and daughters of Israelite families to marry the non-Israelite heathen living around them. Ezra and Nehemiah are a classical case study in the Bible against interracial marriage.

It is important to remember that when *Jehovah* separated Israel from the Adamic nations (Deuteronomy 32:8-9), He intended Israel to be a separated people unto Himself. Exodus 33:16 and Leviticus 20:24-25 both confirm that Israel was to be a separated people. You cannot read these Scriptures and then believe that God wanted Israel to mix, amalgamate, and mongrelize with other races. Such thinking would be an affront to God and His infallible and unchanging Word. Deuteronomy 7:6-8, 14:2, and 26:16-19, confirm that Israel was to be a special, separated people unto the God of Scripture. Psalm 147:19-20 validates the fact that Israel was given the Law so that they would know how to live differently than the rest of the world. Separa tion, segregation, and racial purity are God's plan for Israel and every other people throughout all of time.

A review of the 7th Commandment in Exodus 20:14 confirms that adultery, in its fullest meaning, includes the prohibition against the destruction of the marriage covenant through race-mixing. The 7th Commandment states, *"Thou shalt not commit adultery."* The very excellent *Brown-Driver-Briggs-Gesenius Lexicon to the Old Testament Hebrew Scriptures* demonstrates that the word *adultery* goes beyond marriage itself and includes idolatrous worship of Baal. The idolatrous worship of Baal included race mixing. Noah Webster's *1828 Dictionary of the English Language* establishes that the word *adulterate* means to corrupt, debase, or make impure by an admixture of baser materials. The English word *adultery*, when studied in the full context of its Hebrew derivation, means that the seventh commandment would safeguard the marriage covenant from interracial marriage or the adulteration of the blood.

The Solution to Miscegenation

Living in a time of history when the typical family, the mainline Churches, and the government have all joined to encourage race-mixing, what can a Christian who wishes to remain true to his Christian conscience do? Please pray about and consider these options:

1) If you are personally involved with an interracial marriage, separate as per Scripture (Ezra 10:18-19). The father should still assume the financial liability for this wife and any mongrel children born to this unholy union.

2) Remove your children from integrated public schools and either home school them (first preference) or place them in a Christian school that contains no unwanted dregs from the public schools (second preference).

3) Move your family to a neighborhood, suburb, or community where you have the greatest concentration of your kind of people living. Cluster with those of like kind and faith.

4) Cultivate a strong fellowship with a Church that follows the Bible with regard to the sin of miscegenation. Do not fellowship in a Church where interracial marriages are condoned and encouraged.

5) Teach your children, work with your children, and be careful that they establish friendships with those of their own kind.

6) Live and worship among those of your own kind, and avoid all conflict and tension with other races.

7) Remember that God created all the races separately and distinctly, that He has a plan and a purpose for every race, and that **you should harbor hatred toward none of God's creation. Resolve to keep your sons and daughters racially pure and Christian in this present world.** Let each follow the pattern established by Noah both with respect to **righteousness of life** and **purity of race. (Genesis 6:6 and Hebrews 11:7).**

Finally, let every God-fearing, Caucasian family know this: America is being inundated with immigrants from the third world. Thousands cross the Mexican border every day seeking a better way of life in America. The Hispanics are now numerically in control of Southern California, Arizona, New Mexico, South Texas, portions of Colorado, and now are moving by the thousands into Northwest Arkansas. The islands of the Caribbean, including Cuba, Haiti, and Puerto Rico, have extended their borders to include all of Florida. Florida and California belong to the third world. Moreover, New York City, along with most every other major metropolitan area of the United States, belongs to the third world.

The Caucasian population of the United States is being overwhelmed in a sea of color. The coastal areas of the United States from Seattle south to San Diego belong to the non-white, third world people. South Texas is becoming a mere extension of Mexico. All of Florida is gone. Only white enclaves remain amid a sea of color. New York City, Detroit, Chicago, Cleveland, St. Louis, Kansas City, Denver, Los Angeles, San Diego, Seattle, Houston, and other major cities are engulfed in a human sea of color. America is no longer a Caucasian nation. The Caucasian race is the minority race in a land where they once held a strong majority. This is a serious day for every Caucasian, Christian family who is concerned for the future of their children. Unless Christian parents make proper decisions today, tomorrow will be too little too late!

I appeal to the Christian conscience of every Christian father and mother who is spiritually alive in Jesus Christ. Now is the hour of decision. What will you do today to insure the future of your children in this country? Unless you take decisive action, your children will be lost amid an ocean of non-whites. Every aspect of life will be affected by this tidal wave of color. The quality of life that your children enjoy will be determined by the steps you take today. May God the Father, God the Son, and God the Holy Ghost, the triune God of Scripture and history, guide your spiritual footsteps in this monumental hour of decision.

12

THE BIBLE CASE AGAINST RACE MIX-ING

"When the Most High divided to the nations their inheritance, when he separated the sons of Adam, he set the bounds of the people according to the number of the children of Israel. For the LORD's portion is his people; Jacob is the lot of his inheritance" (Deuteronomy 32:8-9).

The clergy in contemporary America asserts forthwith that interracial marriage is sanctioned by God and Scripture. Both the pulpit and the pew in most mainstream denominational churches are content with the miscegenation mania that is rampant throughout the landscape of America. A vast majority of the American clergy, representing a cross section of almost every major denomination in the Christian world, stands resolutely in favor of interracial marriage. Interracial dating, marriage, and social interaction are now commonplace throughout America. Every college and university campus in the land is a test tube for interracial dating, live-in relationships, and interracial marriage.

The idea of interracial dating and marriage is commonplace not only in the public schools, colleges, and universities of our country, but also in the churches. In 1967, the Supreme Court voided state bans on interracial marriage.

From this point forward, interracial marriage became commonplace in the church. Miscegenation, once scorned in the church and forbidden by statutory law, then became accepted behavior throughout America. The rush to integrate the homes of America is now on. Anyone who opposes this unbiblical practice is considered intolerant and bigoted.

Ministers stand on their theological hands trying to prove from the Bible that God approves of interracial marriage. They push Scripture out of context, violate every law of Bible hermeneutics, and wrangle and twist every law of Scripture in an effort to place God's blessing on race mixing. We have reached the point where vast numbers of stalwart Christian people are retreating from the time-honored practice of opposing race mixing. More and more people are willing to compromise this vital truth in an effort to find peace in the face of this terrible sin. In an effort to salve their spiritual consciences, people have commissioned their pastors to do what is necessary to prove a Bible case in favor of race mixing.

Remnant ministers, one by one, are falling into the established mindset on interracial marriage. The first step toward accepting interracial marriage is teaching that Jesus Christ died for the entire world. If He died for all races without exception and all races find salvation in Jesus Christ, then it is a quick and easy trip to a biological union of all races. If we are all spiritual equals in Jesus Christ, it is easy to justify biological fusion in the marriage covenant. Little by little, remnant ministers are erasing the battle line against race mixing. Those who seek compromise at this vital point of truth will spare nothing in their effort to erase this important Bible truth. They will wrest Scripture, wrangle and debate, and exalt human reason above all the Word of God to make room for a fully integrated congregation. Finally, as their consciences become seared with the hot iron of human reason and compromise, they blaspheme the altar of the living God by solemnizing a marriage between blacks and whites or any other combination of races.

It is appalling to examine the limits that Bible teachers will go to in their efforts to make a place in Scripture for interracial marriage. Every Scripture in the Bible is carefully scrutinized to make room for race mixing. These false apostles of Satan's kingdom will do anything to make it appear that the Word of God commends race mixing. If you believed what the modern clergy preach, you would believe that Adam and Eve might have been black and white. You would believe that Asenath, wife of Joseph, and Zipporah, wife of Moses, and other leading women of the Scripture were black or some color other than white. The American clergy appears to derive some special pleasure out of turning the Holy Bible into a racial polyglot of twisted and confusing bloodlines that end up merging all races into one fully integrated and mingled people. These preachers of mix and mate, love and amalgamate go to any end to promote interracial dating, marriage, and social relationships.

This miscegenation mania at the pulpit, in the pew, throughout mainstream America, and now appearing in the remnant pulpit is cause for grave concern. **Blood pollution is forever; it's irreversible!** We can rebuild the foundations of a collapsed economy. The rotting political infrastructure of America can be restored amid fasting, prayer, and Bible study. A resolution for our social problems can, in time, be found. But if we pollute our blood amid the sin of miscegenation and reduce the purity of the Caucasian and every other race to a bland gray, America will be finished forever. Every base nation on earth today results from the fusion of the primary builder race with the other races.

The browning of Egypt, Greece, North Africa, India, Peru, and other nations resulted from race mixing. Those who fail to live by the Biblical Law of racial purity will be judged in the eternal loss of the genetic foundations upon which nations are built.

Race mixing in modern America arises from several false premises which are communicated from the pulpit and the pew, plus premises that incessantly are propagated from the public schools, colleges, and universities of this land. A quick review of the false presuppositions that undergird the mindset of the American public, and Christians in particular, is in order.

THE "UNITY OF ALL RACES" DOGMA

American pulpits are ablaze with the theory that all races had a common beginning in Adam and Eve. They assert that there is a unity of all races in Adam man. Building on this postulate, they conclude that since all races had a common beginning with Adam, nothing is wrong with the fusion, integration, and amalgamation of all races into one, gray polyglot. The unity of the races concept is built directly from the theory of evolutionary humanism. Theological evolution as preached from American pulpits asserts that all the diverse races have resulted from mutations from one original parent stock in Adam and Eve. This "unity of all races" dogma allows ministers to read the Bible with color blind vision. Most of the clergy imagine God to be color blind, and they see the Bible as a book of integrated bloodlines with no provision for any racial purity.

Many theologians trace the origin of the races to the post-flood history of Genesis and contend that from Noah's three sons, Shem, Ham, and Japheth, sprang the three major races of the earth: the Caucasian, Negroid, and Oriental races. Since they trace all major races to a common beginning in Noah, they see nothing inherently wrong in the mixing of the races. Most of the clergy, together with their congregations, have joined educators and politicians in the clamor to mix and shake, amalgamate and integrate all races into one fusion of gray. The doctrine of evolutionary humanism has made its way to the American pulpits, and the pews are ripe with the same dogma. As in the days of Hosea the prophet, *"my people are destroyed for lack of knowledge" (Hosea 4:6)*. While most Christians would not admit that they have built their ideas about race upon the foundations of evolution, it nevertheless is true. **Charles Darwin and the doctrine of evolution have found an enduring place in contemporary America.**

At this late date, it is not likely that anyone will be able to change the thinking of the masses in America and the Israelite nations abroad. Interracial dating, marriage, and socialization are accelerating throughout the Western world. The non-white races of the third world have invaded the nations of the West, and the Caucasian Christians can hardly wait to bring these people into the churches and down the altar where interracial marriages can be solemnized. At the very best, we can only pray that as the Scripture says (Isaiah 1:9 and Romans 11:5), there will be a remnant of racially pure Israelites spared to the coming of Jesus Christ in power and glory.

The time has come for the remnant to draw lines from the Bible for themselves and their children. We should build from a foundation of Bible truth and transmit this knowledge to our children so a Godly seed can be preserved in the earth during this time of Jacob's Trouble. If the rest of the world chooses to mix, mate, and amalgamate, fine. As for me and my house, however, that is not our choice. We believe that we cannot violate our consciences by living in disobedience to God and Scripture. Interracial dating, marriage, and social interaction are a total violation of God and His Law and clearly oppose the historic position of the Christian Church.

As Christians we can solicit no conflict or tension with other races or with people who are obsessed with race mixing. We are content to view the presence of non-whites in America as a judgment upon Caucasian America for violating God's Word. We accept the fact that the third world is arriving in America because the Israelite people have broken covenant with *Jehovah*, their God. The presence of foreign, alien people in America in increasing numbers is no great mystery. Scripture is clear that persistent violation of the covenant Law of God by the Israelite people will result in the alien conquest of their land. The arrival of millions of non-white aliens into the American Fatherland in the last half of the 20th century is more than sufficient reason for all who will be Christian to turn in repentance to their God. Our prayer is that the Christian remnant can be spared a place for themselves and their children in a land that is becoming home to the third world.

SEPARATION AND DISTINCTION

We believe that every race was created distinct from all others by the sovereign will of God. Each race, with its own unique and distinctive color of skin, blood composition, mental abilities and limitations, and other attributes, bears the mark of Divine ownership. Every race was created by God and was pronounced very good (Genesis 1:31). Every race bears the original design of God in skin color and all other unique qualities established by the act of creation. The Christian view must be that every race has its particular life purpose in the plan of God. Moreover, it must be true that what God created perfect in the beginning will be a part of His Kingdom design in the end. We believe that every race as created in its pristine, original design will be resident within the Kingdom when Jesus Christ rules this earth. Every race will occupy that portion of the earth assigned to them by their God. There can be no hatred for the various races that the Creator has created and placed upon His earth.

It is imperative that every Christian understand how it is that interracial dating, marriage, and socialization of the race destroy God's mark of ownership and destroy God's original design for every race as purposed in creation. Miscegenation is mortal man seeking to remake God's creation into his own image. Race mixing is the attempt of sinful man to recreate that which God called very good. Every act of miscegenation is man's attempt to exalt the god of human reason above the intent and purpose of the Creator God. Miscegenation is an abomination before God. All who practice and wallow in this sin must love death.

VALUE AND FUNCTION IN RACE

It is important to establish the difference between value and function in the races which God has created. As to God's perception of value, we are not allowed to pass judgment. Every race has a definite purpose in the will of the Creator. God placed value on every race. Therefore, no race is considered valueless. That the Creator found all races to be very good indicates that we are not at liberty to assign value. The Creator loves all of His creation, and so should His children. As to function, every race has a particular and unique position to fill in the purpose and plan of God; no two races were created to fill the same function. When mortal man seeks to assign the various races to the same function and position, there is no end to the problems that ensue. You must clearly separate value from function among the various races God created.

The sin of miscegenation assumes that because every race has value in the sight of God, they all share the same function and position in the plan of the Creator. Interracial cohabitation brings death to both function and value in racial purity. By changing God's original design and re-making the race in the image of Satan, both function and value are destroyed. Failure to understand function in race has resulted in making demands on a particular race which it cannot deliver. The Creator has placed His own limitations on each race, and no amount of wishful thinking and social planning will change this fact. Not every race was designed for the same function, and when forced to perform beyond their limitations, chaos follows. Only when God's original design is protected in every race will peace and harmony be present.

KIND AFTER HIS KIND

The Law of Kind after His Kind is established ten times in Genesis one. Every life form in the plant and animal world was created after his kind, with seed in itself. The distinct races within God's creation were created to conform to the law of kind after his kind. Caucasians were created to reproduce in kind. Negroids were created to reproduce in kind. Orientals were created to procreate within their own kind. The same law that keeps blackbirds reproducing after their own kind is intended to keep each race reproducing after his own kind. In thousands of years of history, the Law of Kind after His Kind has operated in the plant and animal world. Only under conditions forced by the hand of man are hybrid crossbreeds possible.

Miscegenation is a total violation of this law. The hybrid offspring of out of kind reproduction has no place in God's creation. Race mixing brings confusion of face. The destruction of the genes is permanent in race mixing. If only the people of this generation would spend as much time in selecting mates for their children as they spend in selective breeding of their dogs, cats, horses, and other animals, we would be in much better condition!

THE LIVING CREATURES

Genesis 1:24-25 provides the Biblical context for the separate and distinct creation of the black and yellow races. The Bible treats the Negroid and Oriental races under the term *living creature* (Chay Nephesh). The Bible does not particularize the life forms of the plant and animal world or the black and yellow races. Each race was created according to his kind and was to reproduce within kind. The preservation of a distinct Oriental race and a distinct Negroid race over thousands of years confirms that there is a natural proclivity for every race to produce after its own kind. The Bible does not teach that Adam and Eve were the parents of all races. Every race had its own distinctive beginning. There is nothing in all of Scripture that teaches a unity of all races in Adam man. The Bible teaches just the reverse. It is no disgrace to be classified under the term living creature. Remember that God called everything that He had made very good, and that included all of the various kinds of the living creature.

ADAM KIND CREATION

The Holy Scriptures take special care to particularize the creation of Adam kind in Genesis 1:26-27. Adam man, unlike the other races, was created in the image and likeness of God and was created with all the attributes requisite and necessary to fulfill the dominion mandate (Genesis 1:28). The incorporeal souls of Adam kind (male and female) were all created on the sixth day (Genesis 1:27). These souls were created in the image and after the likeness of the

Creator God and were given all of the unique qualities, talents, and gifts necessary to bring forth their function in the earth. With regard to function, the Adamic creation was given the dominion of the earth.

The first body form created in Adamic man was the man Adam in Genesis 2:7. Adam was the first body into which a created soul was placed (Genesis 2:7). The soul became living in the sense that it now possessed self-consciousness. The soul possessed only God consciousness in Genesis 1:27. With the breath of life (Genesis 2:7), Adam man was made living. This breath of life was the spirit of life (Job 27:3). Adam man was made spirit, soul, and body (I Thessalonians 5:23). He had a created, incorporeal (non-material) soul, a formed body (Genesis 2:7), and an implanted spirit (Genesis 2:7). Adam, made in the likeness and after the image of God, was created to exercise dominion over the earth (Genesis 1:28, Genesis 9:1, and Psalm 8).

Adam man was the first Caucasian to be placed in a body with an implanted spirit (Genesis 2:7). All of the souls of Adam man (male and female) that ever were to be born in time and creation were created on day six (Genesis 1:26-27). On day eight, the created soul of Adam was placed into a formed body (Genesis 2:7) and was given an implanted spirit, which gave him life (James 2:26). The form and function of the first man was to be reproduced in kind by Adam and his posterity. The Bible declares itself to be the history of the Adamic people (Genesis 5:1-3). Moreover, the word *man* in Genesis 1:26,27 and Genesis 2:7 is word #120, *Aw-Dawm'*, from #119, meaning ruddy, i.e. a human being (an individual or the species, mankind, etc) man, person. Root #119 is *Aw-Dam'*, to show blood in the face, flush or turn rosy, be (dyed, made) red (ruddy). Genesis 1:26-27 and Genesis 2:7 both speak of the creation of Adam man. Moreover, Genesis 5:1-3 and Matthew 19:4-6 confirm that the language of Genesis 1:26-27 and 2:24 speaks of one creation: Adam man.

From the creation of Adam sprang the Caucasian race. When it became necessary for Adam to find a help meet (wife), he found nothing acceptable within the other races present in the creation. Genesis 2:20 reveals that there was not an help meet found for Adam man. The Law of Kind after His Kind was validated when God took Eve out of the side of Adam man. Genesis 2:24 confirms that the man and the woman are to be of *one flesh*, that is, the same *kind* of flesh. The fact that Adam man did not find himself a wife from another race confirms that Adam man must always find a wife of his own flesh. In Adam and Eve we have the first progenitors of the Adamic creation. The soul of Eve was created on day six right along with the soul of Adam (Genesis 1:26-27). The soul of the woman was placed into the body which God formed when He took out of Adam's side a rib with which to make a woman. The woman Eve was made in kind after Adam man. This is the Bible bedrock foundation for preserving the racial integrity of the race of Adam.

The race of Adam was placed under the blessing and cursing of the Law in Genesis 2. Obedience to the commands of the Creator would insure Adam's immorality. He would never die. Disobedience to the commands of His Creator would bring forth death. Adam enjoyed conditional immortality. When sin entered the world and death by sin (Romans 5:12), the race of Adam lost its innocence and joy before God and was cast from the Garden of Eden. Following their expulsion from Eden, the Garden of God, the Adamic creation continued to practice racial integrity by remaining within the law of kind after his kind. This cannot be said with regard to Cain. In Genesis 4, Cain took a wife from the land of Nod (a member of the Oriental race), and this was the beginning of the sinful plunge into race mixing.

ISRAEL OUT OF ADAM

Only Adam man was placed under Law (Genesis 2). The other races were not made responsible for keeping the Law and therefore were not held accountable unto the Creator. Where there is no law, there is no transgression (Romans 4:15). Moreover, sin is not imputed where there is no law (Romans 5:13). In the fall of man into sin, only the Adamic creation stood under the sentence of death and judgment. Only Adam kind required redemption from sin. The other races were under the headship of Adam kind. The entire creation suffered and groaned in travail because of original sin, because Adam man was responsible for the Godly dominion of all creation. When Adam sinned, the entire creation suffered. Only the Adamic race sinned, however, and that sentence of death required a Savior who could reconcile them back into right standing with God the Father.

God the Father was under no obligation to save anyone since He was not responsible for Adam man's fall into sin. Out of His great love and mercy, the Father purposed in election to choose a people who would be the object of His love (Exodus 19:5,6, Deuteronomy 7:6, Psalms 135:4, Jeremiah 31:1, Amos 3:2, I Peter 1:1,2, James 1:1, and Matthew 15:24). This He did from the foundation of the world (Eph. 1:4,5 & II Tim. 1:9). God the Father purposed to choose Israel out of Adam. Every Israelite is an Adamite, but not every Adamite is an Israelite. Biblical Israel is descended from Adam through Abraham, Isaac, Jacob-Israel, and his twelve sons. From Genesis 12 to the remainder of the New Testament, the Bible is the history of Israel, the people descended from father Abraham through his son Isaac.

In preserving the purity of the Israelite people out of the race of Adam kind, God the Father purposed for Abraham to marry his half sister, Sarah. (They shared the same father). This selective mating was continued with Isaac when he married his cousin Rebekah. Jacob continued this pattern of selective mating when he went to his uncle Laban to seek a wife. Careful examination of the Israelite people will confirm that selective mating was always a part of their history. From the very beginning with Adam and Eve, there people would be of the same flesh (Genesis 2:24). This practice was continued in the unfolding generations, and every violation of the law of racial purity brought sorrow and displeasure (Genesis 26:34-35, 27:46).

Purveyors of mix, mate, and amalgamate would have you believe that Asenath, wife of Joseph, was not white. They want you to believe that Zipporah, wife of Moses, was non-white. They insist that Rachab, wife of Salmon, was non-white. They claim that Ruth, wife of Boaz, was not racially pure. In truth, however, Asenath, Zipporah, Ruth, and other controversial women of the Bible were of the Caucasian race and did descend from Father Abraham. People with a race mixing mentality search every crevice and canyon of the Bible for justification of the sin of miscegenation. When they are honest with the Word of God, they find that the case for miscegenation cannot be defended from the Holy Scriptures.

Finally, let it be noted that in the original design of our Eternal God, he allotted to the various races within His creation a special portion of the earth. He placed the Orientals in Asia, the largest continent on earth. He placed the Negroids in equatorial Africa where the climate is best suited for this creation. He placed the Caucasian race in Europe, in the northern latitudes where they are best suited to carry forth their function in the creation. The integration of the various races in the landscape of America, the Dominion of Canada, the British Isles, Scandinavia, Europe, Australia, New Zealand, So. Africa and elsewhere on this earth cannot be defended from the Bible. The God of Scripture is a God of segregation and separation. What God has segregated, let not man integrate.

If a majority of the Caucasian race in America makes the unscriptural choice to mix, mate, amalgamate, and destroy the treasure and blood of their race in miscegenation, fine. They have to live with that decision. However, we at the Church of Israel have chosen to remain faithful to the covenant Law of God and Scripture. We seek no tension and conflict with other races. We wish that every race would remain faithful to the standards of racial purity. What we seek for ourselves we also wish for all other races. Every race should seek to preserve the **original design** of the Creator. Race mixing will erase God's mark of ownership. When persons of any race engage in interracial dating and marriage, they have crossed one of the very most important lines drawn by God and Scripture. Those who do so have taken a step into the darkness of night. This tragic walk will harvest bitter fruit, sorrow, pain, and suffering in this world, and in the world to come, eternal damnation.

May the God of Heaven grant to the Christian remnant the resolute will and courage to preserve their ethnic integrity for this and future generations. We do not have to forfeit our racial heritage by jumping into the sewer of miscegenation. Let us look to the God of Abraham, the God of Jacob, and the God of Isaac. *Jehovah*, He is God! May God be praised for those who, by faith in Jesus Christ, will seek to preserve the spiritual and racial purity of their family and Church.

13

THE MILLION MAN MARCH

October 16, 1995, will be recorded as a significant day in American history. On this day, the largest gathering of black males in the history of the United States massed in Washington D. C. The United State's Park Service estimated the crowd at about 450,000 black persons, but other reputable sources placed the figure at 850,000 or more. Close to one million black males assembled; this gathering was considerably larger than the previous record set by the followers of Martin Luther King Jr. in the 1960's. The million man march was called by **Louis Farrakhan,** leader of the black Muslims. Farrakhan is the notorious black Muslim leader who has consistently blasted the Jews, spoken openly against Caucasians, and has called for a separate black nation within the United States. For years he has been denied any reputable standing by any political party in the United States, and the News Media has never given him any slack. All of the above may be under review in light of the charisma that Farrakhan seems to have with black America.

This massive gathering of black males was called the black man's **Day of Atonement.** It was to be a time of prayer, repentance, and atonement by the black males for their long failures with the family in rearing their children, failure in the work place, and a general lack of responsibility. It was also a call for voter registration among blacks throughout America and an exhortation for black resurgence in both the market place and the political future of America. Blacks of all political/social/economic status attended, with prevailing numbers from the more educated segment of the black male population of America. The mass gathering was most impressive, especially in view of the notorious history and leadership of Louis Farrakhan.

Several significant factors need to be mentioned about this march on Washington D. C. Firstly, the Democratic Party distanced itself from a major black event for the first time in this century. In all previous occasions, white liberals from the Democratic Party could be counted on to play a major role. On this occasion, however, white liberals distanced themselves from the march and sought to keep the Democratic Party isolated from any association with the mass gathering. Secondly, white liberals of every stripe and political persuasion were silent and without commitment in their support of the march or of the leadership of Louis Farrakhan. Thirdly, the American news media, both television and the newspapers, tip-toed around the march, making no effort to expose Louis Farrakhan or the vision that he has for a black separatist, Muslim state within the United States.

Remnant Christians should be alerted to the potential signals that this march has demonstrated. It would be tragic if remnant Christians failed to learn valuable lessons from this march. Consider the potential developments that are clearly visible in light of this mass gathering of black males in Washington D. C.

1) The fact that Louis Farrakhan could command such a large number of black males, on such short notice, and

without a serious event to provoke the black community, to gather in Washington D. C. is of great importance.

2) That so many black males could come together under the leadership of Louis Farrakhan is also significant in light of his notorious beliefs. Farrakhan is an avowed Muslim; he has spewed great hatred toward the Jewish Community and has consistently called for a separate, black Muslim state within the United States. In addition, Farrakhan has sought to awaken the black population of America to their alleged mistreatment in the days of slavery.

3) The march has demonstrated that the news media in America operates under two standards: one for those calling themselves white separatists, and another for those calling themselves black separatists. No mention is ever made about Louis Farrakhan being a black separatist, while the news media could never mention the name of Randy Weaver without using the words *white separatist*. The American news media considers black separatism to be acceptable, while at the same time it condemns those who call for white separatism.

4) This mass demonstration of black males shows great polarization of the races in America. The melting pot is not melting nearly so well as the social engineers intended. Racial fragmentation is apparent in contemporary America. Black solidarity was well demonstrated in the million man march led by Louis Farrakhan. America shows strong signs of fragmenting along racial polarization.

5) The Democratic Party may no longer contain the demands of a growing black political resurgence. White liberals may no longer be able to satisfy the future political ambitions of millions of black Americans. The black political agenda may be more than the established political par-

ties can accommodate. The mass march may have demonstrated a new future for the black community residing in the United States.

6) White liberals may be forced out of their racist closets by the likes of Louis Farrakhan and other radicals within the ranks of those calling for black political empowerment. Suppressed racism may eventually surface among even white liberals as the surging black millions seek to make radical moves that threaten the security of the upper white middle classes in American society.

7) The million man march has demonstrated solidarity among the more educated blacks. It confirmed the willingness of millions of black males to stand together. If a day of black atonement for their past failures could draw hundreds of thousands of their kind to the nation's capitol, how many would march if there were a real catalyst to fire them up? It is more than apparent that millions of black males are ready to take to the streets to claim power in this nation.

8) The million man march has affirmed the growing tension and hostility that is potentially ready to burst forth among the black population in America. Is America prepared to withstand a black uprising that would number into the millions, touch every major city, and witness mass riots, burning, looting, and violence? The inner cities of America are becoming tinder kegs, ready to explode into racial violence. Is America prepared to endure such an internal racial explosion?

9) The white middle class in America is ill-prepared for the racial conflict that may be apparent on the national scene. Millions of white middle and upper class Americans are unarmed and without any means of protecting themselves against social upheaval. The unending progressive

registration, licensing, and confiscation of firearms in America will leave innocent, law abiding Caucasians help- less to defend themselves, while criminal elements will have armed themselves to the teeth. Millions of these weapons will end up in the hands of the surging black inner city population.

10) The mass drug addiction within the inner city black population has already turned many of the larger urban areas into armed camps. Street gangs now control many of the inner black cities of America. The masses are ripe for rioting, plunder, fire, and looting of the urban areas of America. Local police forces are not able to control and contain street gangs, drug houses, and the traffic in alcohol, crime, and murder within the inner cities of America. If they cannot police these inner cities under present circum- stances, what will they do if rioting, burning, plunder, and armed violence erupt in the major cities of America?

11) Millions of blacks are locked into the American welfare system. For several successive generations, the black population of America's great urban centers have become dependent upon welfare handouts. The inner black popu- lation centers have been contained only because of the monthly welfare checks, food stamps, and urban housing provided by the tax payers of the United States. When the welfare checks, food stamps, and government housing are no longer available, millions of blacks will rise up in the inner cities and move toward the white suburbs. Rioting, plunder, looting, and criminal violence will turn the great American suburbs into burning caldrons.

12) The Caucasian population of America is not ready for any major racial uprising in America. A vast majority of the Caucasian population will suffer tremendous hardship and loss of life in any future racial upheaval that may take

place in the urban areas of our land. The typical white person is unprepared mentally, spiritually, and physically to endure the kind of suffering that will be turned loose when American cities go up in flames. No one will be able to say that a **warning** was not sounded. The danger signs are all present in contemporary America. Violent street gangs, armed and infested with drugs, alcohol, and weapons, now rule many of the inner cities of America. The welfare system in the United States has subsidized millions of black children born out of wedlock. Many black women have no idea who fathered their children. The law of the jungle operates in urban America. Moreover, this immoral jungle life style is beginning to infect the lower and middle class white population of America.

The time has come for the Caucasian Christian remnant to put their best intellectual and spiritual talents together for mutual survival in the days and years ahead. The following summary, gleaned from careful reading of the Holy Scriptures, prayer, meditation, and in counsel with a wide range of people over many years is herein offered to the reader.

WHAT CAN WE DO?

1) Covenant, combine, and separate with others of your kind who share a mutual standard of spiritual, religious, doctrinal, and moral principles. Both faith and race are indispensable in any effort to covenant, combine, and separate yourselves from the mixed multitude now gathering in America. More than mere faith and race will be required for survival. The covenant community must share a close moral, spiritual, and doctrinal value system.

2) People must covenant and combine to separate themselves into rural areas where they can become independent property owners, cultivate gardens, know animal husbandry,

and attend to basic survival needs. People must be prepared to live through some mean, difficult times. It will be a matter of satisfying basic needs. Most people will need to postpone their wants for a better day.

3) Above all, people will need to build a personal relationship with Jesus Christ, live in the Word, cultivate prayer, live by the moral absolutes of Scripture, and love their neighbor. Prepare spiritually, mentally, and physically to survive some hard times. The future belongs to those who fear God, obey His law, love one another, and trust their future to the providence of a sovereign and caring God.

14

RACIAL COMPOSITION OF AMERICA

1607-1995

Some 388 years have passed since the first Caucasian settlers from England arrived in America to establish Jamestown Colony. In almost ten generations, America has passed from an exclusive Caucasian nation of Christian people with high moral standards to a multi-racial nation with no moral standards whatsoever. In the 168 years that passed between the settlement of Jamestown, Virginia (1607) and the opening rounds of the War for Independence (1775), America received the primary influx of Caucasian people from the British Isles with a small percentage coming from other Caucasian nations of Europe. In 1780, more than three of every four Americans were descendants of English and Irish settlers with the balance coming from the Netherlands, France, Germany, and Switzerland. Fewer than 1,000,000 immigrants entered the country from 1790 to 1840. (See *World Book Encyclopedia*, 1960, p. 77).

Population figures are somewhat lacking for the United States prior to 1820 when the United States Census Bureau began to keep records. Between 1841 and 1860, 4,311,465 Caucasian people arrived in America from Ireland, Germany, Great Britain, and France. Political unrest, famine, economic duress, and revolution in Europe made America seem like a haven. By 1860, thirteen out of every 100 people in America had recently arrived from Europe. This wave of immigrants is sometimes known as the "old immigration." (See *World Book Encyclopedia*, 1960, p. 77). By the beginning of the Civil War, America was populated by about twenty-eight million Caucasians from Europe and about 3.5 million blacks. It should be noted that from the beginning of American history to 1868, in the post-Civil War Reconstruction Era of history, only free white men could vote. No non-white person was considered a citizen of the United States of America before passage of the 14th Amendment in 1868.

From Jamestown (1607) to the year 1880, America was peopled by Caucasian people coming from the British Isles, Europe, and Scandinavia. From 1820 to 1860, ninety-five percent of immigrants to America originated in Northern and Western Europe. (See *Inter-Change, Population Reference Bureau*, Inc. Vol. 4, No. 3, Sept. 1975).

These millions of Caucasians came from the Christian culture of Europe, were racially pure, and were a Christian people with high moral standards and a strong work ethic of self-discipline, initiative, thrift, pride, skilled workmanship, and honesty.

Beginning in 1880, and with increased numbers thereafter, a new wave of immigration began in the United States. In 1882, three of every four immigrants came from Northern and Western Europe. But, by 1896, more than half the immigrants were coming from countries in Southern and Eastern Europe, including Italy and Austria-Hungary. (See *World Book Encyclopedia*, 1960, p. 77). This massive wave of immigration from Southern and Eastern Europe became known as the "new immigration" and included thousands of Khazarian Mongolian Jews who came to the United States with hostile feelings toward the Christian culture of this country. 1880 marked the beginning of the entry of tens of thousands of people, primarily Khazarian Jews, who could not be assimilated into the Christian culture of America. The culture of these people being non-Christian in every sense, there simply was no assimilation of these people into the American culture.

The government of the United States began to control immigration into America in 1882 under pressure from the American public and Labor Unions, and in 1886, Congress halted Chinese immigration into the United States. In 1907, a "gentleman's agreement" between the United States and Japan halted the unlimited immigration of Japanese laborers because of pubic pressure on the Pacific Coast. (See *World Book Encyclopedia*, 1960). Between 1900 and 1910, the flood of immigrants from Southern and Eastern Europe continued to arrive in the United States. In the early 1900's, seven of every ten immigrants were coming from Southern and Eastern Europe. In 1907, the United States admitted a record number of 1,285,349 immigrants. (See *World Book Encyclopedia*, 1960). By the advent of the First World War (1914), America was the dumping grounds for millions of Southern and Eastern Jews and other people who could not be absorbed into the Caucasian Christian culture of the United States.

In 1860, only a tiny trickle of immigrants had arrived in the United States from Southern and Eastern Europe. By 1930, fifty-eight percent of all immigration to America was coming from Southern and Central Europe. (*Inter-Change Population Reference Bureau*, Inc. Vol. 4, No. 3. Sept. 1975). In 1921, the United States Congress passed a quota law which limited the number of immigrants for the first time. This law was especially aimed at Central and Eastern Europe. In 1929, the National Origins Law went into effect and was designed to prevent any major change in the racial composition of the American population. This law established a limit of 150,000 immigrants a year. (See *World Book Encyclopedia*, 1960, p. 77). The National Origins Law emphasized an immigrant's country of origin rather than the country he lived in when he applied for a Visa, and excluded some races, notably Asians. (See *World Book Encyclopedia*, 1960, p. 77). This law, together with the Great Depression of the 1930's, almost halted immigration into the United States at that time.

Beginning in 1945 (during the Post World War II years), America again became the receiving center for hundreds of thousands of immigrants. Under the Displaced Persons Acts of 1948 and 1950, more than 400,000 people entered the United States from Europe, many of them Khazarian Jews. Then in 1952, Japan was given the same immigration quotas as the European countries. The Immigration and Nationality Act of 1952 revised existing immigration laws and grouped all immigration and nationality acts in one basic statute. All of these steps initiated the flood tide of Asians immigrating to this country. The Refugee Relief Act of 1953 further opened our doors for non-whites from Asia and third world countries. By 1971-1974, forty-one percent were coming from Asia, sixteen percent from South and Central Europe, and only a meager six percent from Northern and Western Europe, the seedbed for American immigration from 1607 to 1880. (*War Cycles, Peace Cycles*, Richard Kelly Hoskins, Copyright 1985, p. 58).

Beginning with the Immigration Act of 1965, the flood gates were opened wide, and all restrictions based upon national origins were set aside. Since then, America has become the dumping ground for multiplied millions of non-whites from every corner of the world. To understand what has happened to the racial composition of America since

1945, and with greater emphasis since 1965, is almost beyond human calculation. This results from the following factors, all of which must be evaluated carefully: 1) changing immigration laws which favor non-whites and actually exclude the original white European population from immigrating to America, 2) the illegal entry of millions of Hispanics, Asians, and other immigrants--clear violation of existing immigrations laws, 3) improper counting by the U.S. Census Bureau (No government agency is capable of obtaining an accurate count of the American population), 4) the classification status of the U.S. Census Bureau is in a state of flux, and no one can be sure who is and who isn't white, 5) the high fertility rate of non-whites is exploding, 6) the low fertility rate of the white population is creating minus zero population growth among whites, 7) inter-racial marriage is now socially acceptable and encouraged often at nearly every level of society, 8) the political one-man, one-vote principle of a democracy favors unlimited immigration to the U.S., 9) lack of Bible teaching has fostered such massive ignorance among Caucasian people that they are incapable of acting in the face of racial suicide now occurring, and 10) a lack of historical understanding of racial heritage among American Caucasians has brought about a total state of apathy, ignorance, and a complete breakdown in the moral consciousness of the people.

Since 1970, Mexico has moved her border a thousand miles to the North, and some fifty to sixty million Hispanics now reside in America. Since multiplied millions are illegal--no one knows the exact count. The Spanish language is competing with English to become the primary language of the Southwestern United States. The Hispanic, Asian, and Negroid population now dominates California, Arizona, New Mexico, South Texas, and all of Florida. The racial character of America has undergone dramatic changes since the end of the II World War, and no one can be certain what the total percentage of the non-white population now is in America, except to say that the black-yellow-brown coalition is becoming the primary population base in the United States.

The racial problem in America has now reached a state of acute crisis. A clear and present danger threatens the Caucasian population of the United States. America is now under invasion, and the invaders now occupy major cities and communities in this country. Our college and university campuses are becoming non-white population centers, and non-whites crows our streets and market places. They fill our factories and civil service jobs. America is rapidly becoming a non-white nation. Very quickly now, this changing racial trend will mean that America will emerge as a non-white nation, bankrupt of all Christian morals and poverty-stricken. America is rapidly becoming a third world nation with severe economic decline, poverty, and loss of moral values. Without question we are in the death phase of the western Christian culture. May our Eternal God, through Jesus Christ, grant the Christian remnant a measure of grace to endure and hold their racial and spiritual foundations in place until our King arrives.

15

HISTORICAL CRITERIA FOR RACIAL PURITY

As Christian Israelites, we should examine the historical records for precedents on maintaining racial purity in the family of God. One way of examining racial purity was the **blush test**, used in Spain in the late fifteenth century to eliminate from the Caucasian population Jews and other mixed breeds. In this blush test, one was required to raise the sleeve where there was no possibility of sunburn, and if the veins were clearly blue and visible, one was a **blue blood.** This has been used at various and sundry times in history, and it should be noted that one of the Hebrew root meanings for the word *Adam* means to show blood in the fact, to flush or turn rosy, be red or ruddy (See *Strong's Exhaustive Concordance to the Bible* for *man* as in Genesis 1:26 and Genesis 2:7). One of the racial characteristics of the Caucasian race is the ability to blush.

In early America, classification according to race was based upon the threefold criteria of the blood of the particular individual, his ancestry, and his appearance. In an examination of the blood of a particular individual, various tests were used to determine if that person had a certain percentage of blood from a different race in his veins. In

Louisiana, it was determined that as much as **1/32 Negroid blood** resulted in being designated Negroid by race. Thus, a person appearing perfectly white in skin color, but who had as much as 1/32 Negroid blood, was still classified as black. In most of the early American states, racial purity was so carefully protected that any ascertainable trace of Negroid blood classified one as black. Not one drop of Negroid blood was permissible because of the tremendous mental, physical, and spiritual gap between the Caucasian race and the Negroid race.

Miscegenation laws were strictly enforced in the early history of America. Race mixing was not tolerated. Ministers were forbidden to solemnize a marriage between a white and Negro or mulatto. Interracial marriage was forbidden by law. Separation of the races was morally legislated by statutory law, and until the post World War II era, these laws were enforced in some areas of the country. It was not until after the Civil Rights Act of 1964 that interracial marriages were allowed to be solemnized in some states of the Union.

Medical research may be able to determine if there is any ascertainable trace of Negroid blood in a white person. If the sickle cell anemia were to show in the blood of a white person, this would indicate the presence of Negroid blood since this particular disease is associated with the Negroid race. Probably, other blood tests exist which also can decipher any mixed blood in a person.

Again, please remember that until 1868, with the passage of the 14th Amendment to the Federal Constitution, only free white males could vote in America. Each state had to carefully determine the basis upon which a Caucasian race classification could be established. Regardless of how fair someone's skin was, any white person with an ascertainable trace of Negroid blood was classified as a Negroid.

The Massachusetts Law of 1705, entitled *An Act For The Better Preventing Of A Spurious Mixed Issue*, stated: **"If any Negro or mulatto shall presume to smite or strike any person of the English or other Caucasian nation, such Negro or mulatto shall be severely whipped at the discretion of the justices before whom the offender shall be convicted,"** and further, **"that none of her Majesty's English or Scottish subjects, nor any other Christian Nation, within this province, shall contract matrimony with any Negro or mulatto; nor shall any person, duly authorized to solemnize marriage, presume to join any such marriage, on pain of forfeiting the sum of fifty pounds."**

The ancestry test, sometimes used in early American history to determine racial classification, worked primarily in terms of a person's eight great grandparents and their racial standing. If all eight great grandparents were white with no ascertainable trace of Negroid blood, a person was considered white. In some cases, a person who was one-eighth Indian was not considered white. That is one great grandparent out of eight! The racial classification of the Virginia Code of the 1950's required that one who was one-sixteenth Indian blood, and possessed no more non-Caucasian blood, must be considered white. Often, the one-eighth test was used for any blood besides Negro (such as Indian) because these people appeared white and were assimilated easily into the community. **(Amendment to the Constitution, James O. Pace, Copyright 1985, p.16).**

In summary, the ancestry test as used in American history limited a person to not being more than one-eighth American Indian or other blood besides Negroid. This test required that all carefully examine their racial status--even to the eight great grandparents.

The appearance test generally was used in combination with the ascertainable blood and ancestry test. Remember that when it is used alone, the appearance test is not always reliable. Because of the relaxed standards which gradually were imposed upon the American (white) populace after the Civil War (1865), and particularly after the Civil Rights Acts of 1964, the appearance test is the most widely used criteria for determining racial purity. Ordinarily, this test combined with the ancestry test will be a reliable method of determining racial purity. Until recent times, the Caucasian family units in America carefully guarded their children from mixed marriages. The infusion of non-white blood into the Caucasian race has developed with the changing moral standards that followed the close of World War II, particularly since 1960.

A word of warning is now in order for all Christian parents seeking to preserve the racial purity of their children and all future generations. The infusion of non-white blood of every kind is now a part of the American historical scene. People live as if they were color blind. Fair skinned daughters from Caucasian families, (many of them claiming to be Christian), now openly court the favor of black football, basketball, and baseball players. Coed dormitories on many college and university campuses are nothing more than a brothel of indescribable moral carnage. Interracial dating, mixing, and mating on college and university campuses are now rampant in the United States of America. American high schools are becoming breeding grounds for the same sinful activity. Vast numbers of mamzers (mongrel) children are now being born in America. The Caucasian race is in process of committing racial suicide! Parents, beware! There is a rising possibility of **non-white blood** finding its way into your family by way of your children. Guard carefully the blood lines into which your sons and daughters marry.

MAINTAINING RACIAL PURITY IN THE FAMILY

Because of the ever growing multi-racial society in America, it is urgent that every Christian Israelite family take immediate steps to insure the racial purity of all members of the family. The task will not be easy since every facet of modern life is geared to promoting a fully integrated, amalgamated society. Government, colleges, universities, public schools, cinemas, newspapers, and television and radio programs are dedicated to promoting a fully integrated America. **The fact remains that in this free and open democratic society, those who wish to remain racially pure have the moral and religious duty to do so.** At this late date, we still are able to live where we want and associate with those with whom we choose.

The Christian family is under heavy obligation to take the following steps: children should be instructed carefully in the Biblical laws of racial purity. They deserve the knowledge of what the Word of God says, and these Bible Laws should be enforced throughout their young lives. Children should not be educated in the public integrated schools, nor should they be forced to attend racially integrated Christian schools. Rather, children should attend racially segregated classes or be home schooled.

It is the responsibility of the parents to select carefully the area where the family lives, and every effort must be made to rear children apart from a multi-racial society, even if it is means sacrifice on the part of the family or parents. Considerable time should be spent in Christian training, and when children are old enough to court or look for a life partner, careful consideration should be given to morally and racially pure associations.

The family should carefully select associations so that they are of like morals and race. We need to seek our own kind! If one must live in the city, work a plan with other families to buy property in the same block and locate in areas where Caucasian families of good moral standing dominate. **Cluster with those of like faith and race.**

Many advocate a migration of covenant people to some point beyond the borders of the United States. Having traveled throughout much of Europe and the British Isles and after careful discussion with those who have traveled extensively in Scandinavia, South Africa, Australia, Argentina, Costa Rica, and elsewhere, I conclude that there is no "safe haven" for whites to settle exclusively. We must learn to make the best use of opportunities that are available in our country. Well selected areas of rural America, near small towns, seem to be the best option for the remnant.

The ability to harness various skilled trades may offer the best employment opportunities for many of our people and enable us to live in rural settings. Small cottage industry and various types of arts and crafts also would help the remnant to be independent of corporate America. A key to the racial and spiritual survival of our people lies in the establishment of an economy that fosters skilled trades, self-employment, home industries, and other economic programs that will enable our people to survive without living in the large metropolitan areas, punching a time clock, and submitting to the life style of the racial masses jammed into the asphalt jungles.

The development of strong Christian families, the growth of private home schooling, and the active pursuit of building the Church are the keys to preserving a Christian Caucasian remnant in America. The family, the Church, and the ability to perform honest work to meet the needs of life will aid in spiritual survival of our Christian remnant. The present multi-racial society not only is morally decadent, but is also moving toward irreversible financial collapse. The moral, spiritual fiber of America is on a par with Sodom and Gomorrah. We are approaching a state of national bankruptcy, both financially and morally; very soon, you can anticipate America becoming a poverty-stricken, third world nation. The Living Church, taking note of this situation, will move quickly to build an ark of spiritual survival and help lead the way in establishing Christian families to prepare for the crisis that is now upon us.

The Christian family, now an endangered species, must take quick and decisive steps to insure the spiritual, moral, and racial survival of their children and future generations. Families must build strong moral and spiritual foundations anchored in a personal relationship with Jesus Christ. The Holy Scriptures must be their daily agenda for life, and they must observe the Holy Sabbath and the annual festivals enumerated in Scripture. Families should place their financial houses in order. Get out of debt, and stay out! Say "good-bye" to credit cards and credit buying; learn to live frugally, without debt.

Families also should practice good health principles and live without dependence upon doctors and drugs. Families who observe the dietary laws of the Bible, practice good nutrition, eat lots of raw food, and avoid a high fat diet will eliminate many of the chronic health problems now afflicting the American populace.

Prepare for the future by building strong and enduring spiritual foundations. Families who live by faith in Jesus Christ, repent from dead works, and live by the standard of God's Laws will survive the test now before us. Families that build their future apart from Jesus Christ and His Word, count the Church as being of no great importance, and concentrate their efforts on earthly goals and will go down the tubes. The spiritual test of the ages is now before us. But, a Christian remnant will survive. That is God's promise.

A SCRIPTURAL AND HISTORICAL CRITERIA FOR MAINTAINING RACIAL PURITY IN THE LIVING CHURCH

The living Church of Jesus Christ must move forth with a plan of racial purity in this time of fusion of the races into one polyglot. Israel must be divided from Adam and from Israel (Romans 9:6). Furthermore, we must be able to discern those who are border-line Israelites in outward appearance. Indeed, what is the *test* for anyone, regardless of how white and fair they are? In response to the growing problem of living in a multi-racial nation, the remnant Church must establish a criteria for preserving the moral and racial standards of the Bible.

The Church must be careful not to become obsessed with debate over eye color, hair composition, cranial structure, the form of the nose, and the degrees of whiteness of the skin. The following guidelines will eliminate the need for self-appointed judges to point the finger at people who, by their standards, are not accepted as Israelite. The Scriptural criteria to follow will enable Israelites to become fruit inspectors instead of eye, nose, ear, hair, skin, finger, and toe specialists. We trust and pray that the following criteria, built from the Word of God and the history of our Caucasian race, will be the means by which the ecclesia of Jesus Christ can sort the Israelites from the Adamites and whereby the mamzers (mongrels) will be sorted from the Living Church, the Body of Christ.

1) Discern them by the fruits they bear. The principle of fruit-bearing is established clearly in the Holy Scriptures. *"Wherefore by their fruits ye shall know them"* is a well marked principle established by Jesus Christ. Carefully study Matthew 7:15-20; 13:23; and John 15:1-17. By their fruits you will know who should be numbered in the Living Church of Jesus Christ.

2) Discern them by preaching and teaching of the Word of God. The Word of God is quick, powerful, and sharper than any two-edged sword, piercing even to the dividing asunder of the soul, spirit, joints, and marrow of the body (Hebrews 4:12). The Word of God will not return unto Him void (Isaiah 55:11). The Word of God, if preached, will be effectual (Romans 10:17), and only Israelites will hear and understand (Romans 9:6; John 10:27-28). The Parable of the Sower is sufficient proof that the sowing (planting) of the Word of God will sort those who are and who are not the Israel of God (Mark 4:14-20).

3) Discern them by their endurance and perseverance in the truth. Those who are the elect will endure and persevere in their faith and calling in Jesus Christ. They will not fizzle out, cop out, melt down, run out, flip flop, flame out, or burn out, but will endure to the end. We are running a race. Who will finish it? The elect in Jesus Christ will finish that pilgrimage called Christian discipleship (Matthew 10:22; I John 2:19; II Peter 2:21,22; Hebrews 12:7,8; James 1:12; Hebrews 6:4-8; 10:26-39; and Job 17:9).

4) Discern them by their character traits. The fruits of the Holy Spirit become the character traits of those Israelites who are called to be Christians. These fruits are enumerated in Galatians 5:22-24: Faith, goodness, gentleness, longsuffering, love, joy, peace, meekness, and temperance. These traits belong to those who are quickened by the Holy Spirit and made alive in Jesus Christ (John 3:3-5). They bring to light the new nature in Jesus Christ, a nature that exhibits the gifts of the Holy Spirit as enumerated in I Corinthians 12:6-11.

5) Discern them by the word of their testimony. If they belong to Jesus Christ, they will stand firmly by the faith once delivered to the saints and will bear a correct and fearless testimony of Jesus Christ, even in trouble and tribulation (I John 4:1-3; II John 7-11; Jude 4, and Revelation 12:11).

6) Discern them by the witness of their Christian living. The daily application of the Christian standards of morality become one of the greatest of all ways to validate a true member of the body of Christ. Those who are able to bear a Christian witness in their daily lives through the application of Christian standards of obedience to God's Holy Law, do, by their sanctified lives, confirm that they are the children of God. Walking in daily obedience to the discipline of Jesus Christ and His Law is a powerful witness to confirm who is and who is not a genuine Christian. Christianity is more than a Sabbath morning experience; it is a way of life. The straight gate is our justification by the blood of Jesus Christ. The narrow way is our walk in sanctification through obedience to God's Law. Those who can talk the talk but cannot walk the walk of Biblical Christianity will be sorted out in the living Church by the election of God our Father.

7) Discern them by the sovereignty of God in election. Romans 8:28-29 confirms that the sovereign will and purpose of God is worked out in the election that was purposed from the foundation of the world. Jesus Christ does claim His own, and He will lose none given Him by the Father. His sheep know Him, and He knows His sheep. The election of God will separate the "sheep" from the "goats" in the baptism of fire. The sifting sands of election grind slowly, but exceedingly fine. The sorting out of the Living Church proceeds on the basis of divine election. God, not man, adds to the Church (Acts 2:47). See Matthew 7:21-

23, Galatians 4:28-31; John 1:12,13; Phil. 2:13; and Romans 9:16, 21.

It is important that those who are called in Jesus Christ and who desire to walk in His marvelous truth beware of walking in **presumptuous judgment.** The Word of God clearly warns against judging a brother or sister in the Body of Christ apart from the truth and spirit of Galatians 6:1. What greater judgment can be handed down than to judge another person to be "racially unfit" for membership in the Living Church? We are warned that when we judge improperly, we ourselves shall be judged. (Matthew 7:1-5; Romans 2:1; Luke 6:37; Romans 14:13; I Corinthians 4:5; and James 4:12). Only those who live faultlessly in terms of the law (and in every point of it) can judge another brother (James 2:9-12; 4:11-12). If you have reason to believe that a person in the Covenant family is not racially pure, take this matter to Jesus Christ in fervent prayer. If you fail to receive the answer through prayer and meditation in the Word, take your case to the pastor/minister in charge. Do not allow your tongue to set a fire among the Body of Christ (James 3:6).

Let every member of the Living Church walk humbly before God and acknowledge the saving power of Jesus Christ in fear and trembling. Many are sifted in the Body of Christ in the fires of tribulation and testing. The fact that one is white does not alone insure entrance into the Kingdom of God. You are not saved for the Kingdom of God because you are born white. Without faith in Jesus Christ, no one can be saved (John 14:6). **Jesus Christ is the only door by which man can receive entrance into the Kingdom of God** (John 3:3-5; 10:7-11; 14:6). All Christians must be judged on the basis of their fruits. Many Israelites who believed themselves devout and everlastingly devoted to the truth will leave that which once they cherished so dearly.

Every Christian needs to study, meditate, and reflect upon the Parable of the Sower. Every living Christian can find where they are in Christ by reading this parable.

As members of the Living Church, let us remember that we are called upon to work out our salvation with fear and trembling (Phil. 2:12). In II Peter 1:10, we are admonished to make our calling and election sure. In Philippians 3:14, we are challenged to press toward the mark for the prize of the High Calling of God in Jesus Christ. Luke 9:62 calls us to take hold of the plow handles and not look back. There is no turning back! We are called to run the race! We must finish our Christian course. We must keep the faith! The Living Church must be preserved morally and racially pure. This is no time to compromise the faith, to be color blind. Open your spiritual eyes! By the unfailing help of Jesus Christ, let us preserve the spiritual, moral, and racial purity of the Living Church.

CPSIA information can be obtained
at www.ICGtesting.com
Printed in the USA
BVOW11s1219291217
504008BV00018B/530/P